Freeing the
Oppressed

Freeing the
Oppressed

A Call to Christians concerning
DOMESTIC ABUSE

Ron Clark

CASCADE *Books* · Eugene, Oregon

FREEING THE OPPRESSED
A Call to Christians concerning Domestic Abuse

Cascade Books
A Division of Wipf and Stock Publishers
199 W. 8th Ave., Suite 3
Eugene, OR 97401

ISBN 13: 978-1-60608-484-7

Cataloging-in-Publication data:

Clark, Ron.

Freeing the oppressed : a call to Christians concerning domestic abuse / Ron Clark.

ISBN 13: 978-1-60608-484-7

xviii + 154 p. ; 23 cm. — Includes bibliographic references and index.

1. Church work with abused women. 2. Abused women—Pastoral counseling of. 3. Church work with abusive men. 4. Abusive men—Pastoral counseling of. I. Title.

BV 4445.5 .C550 2009

Manufactured in the U.S.A.

Contents

Figures

Preface

IT WAS THE third time that I had seen *Forrest Gump*. I don't remember where I was (or why I was watching it for the third time); I just remember the thought that flashed through my mind as I watched one of the scenes. Jenny had come back to see Forrest at his home in Alabama. They went by her old house, which was now abandoned, and she began to get angry. She yelled and threw rocks at the house. That's when I got it. She had been abused as a child! It all came together. Her erratic behavior in the movie, her distant love of Forrest (the only man who truly loved her), and her choices in life were all understandable now. How could I have missed it?

You are probably thinking "Everyone saw it but you—why did you have to watch it three times to get it?" My answer: I don't know. I wonder the same thing. But this helps me to understand why faith communities don't "get it." That's right; sometimes faith communities don't get it. We see the story over and over again until someone grabs us and says, "Mary is being abused, and you have done nothing." Then it makes sense; yet we still might not know what to do about it.

My wife, Lori, and I have been working with abuse victims and shelters since 1992. We have given countless sermons, classes, and trainings on abuse and have helped victims and abusers find resources. In the beginning we served the women, children, and staff at a small safe house in southern Missouri. We felt compelled to help, and we rallied the church to provide pizza parties, build fences (literally) and playground equipment, help with odd jobs for the house, provide clothing and gifts for the children, and offer a safe place for the families to worship. The director of the shelter encouraged us to attend domestic-violence prevention and intervention trainings offered by local service providers and counselors. She later offered us the opportunity to provide counseling and trainings for others in the community as well as the shelter guests. Wherever we are, the memories of the staff and guests in that small safe house, who courageously pushed us to get involved, drive us forward. Sometimes even *we* have to see the movie a third time to get the message. Other times we see it coming but feel we can do nothing about it.

Yet God was not finished with us. When we came to Portland, Oregon, in August 1998, we were introduced to a new view of domestic violence. The abusers I had so hated and ignored became flesh and dwelt among us. I began to attend workshops presented by batterer-intervention specialists and anger-management counselors. I had coffee, lunch, and even dinner in our home with people working daily with this issue. We have spoken together at state, national, and international conferences, and I am amazed at the support I receive from advocates throughout the country. We learned that accountability, change, mercy, and lastly forgiveness needed to become part of our abuse-awareness language. Abusers had always been among us; we had just ignored them and focused on the victims. We learned that when we say, "Mary *was/is abused*" rather than "Steve *abused* Mary," our very language suggests that women are at fault.

I believe that my family lives in one of the best states in the country. Oregon is not only full of natural beauty, but it has excellent domestic-violence intervention programs. I have learned much from the domestic-violence intervention advocates and counselors. The number of opportunities to gather and present research in the area of theology and domestic violence has grown immensely in the Northwest. These advocates have also been willing to listen to and seek advice from this preacher, and I will always remember the times we have prayed together for their work. At our church's annual domestic-violence conference, I introduced a local batterer-intervention trainer to my son as "the man who is teaching me to be a better dad." God has truly used these servants to teach my family how to be more like Jesus. I look forward to what God will continue to do through them in the future.

At times we have felt despair: Despair over the size of this problem and the costs involved in trying to educate the world. Despair over the abuser who clouds the conversation with "no one is perfect, can't you just give me a break?" Despair over the men who continue to use power and control to manipulate their partners, their children, and others around them. Despair over the victims who have come for help, only to return to their abuser. Despair over the children who can't get away. Despair over the churches that tell me, "Thanks, but we have it under control"; or, "It doesn't exist in our church."

I hope this book will help you to "get it" the first time you see it. If you are a church leader, my hope is that you will become an advocate for families that suffer from abuse. If you are a former victim, my hope is that this book will validate your struggle and journey to freedom. If you are a family member or friend of someone who feels the pain of abuse, I hope that you will learn how to be a good listener, helper, and friend. If you are abusing your partner or your wife, my challenge is that you stop, repent of this sin, and enroll in a batter-intervention or anger-management group. I also challenge you to confess this sin to your family, friends, and those you are abusing. This book is designed to help you learn about domestic violence and what it is like to experience abuse. Many victims who have experienced pain have told us their stories. Contrary to what Forest Gump said, life is not always "like a box of chocolates."

A Special Message for Those Being Hurt by Their Partner or Family Member

If you are now being abused or afraid of being hurt by your partner, my hope and prayer is that you will learn how to get help and be safe. My hope is that you will not have to live the life that Jenny lived, and that you will see that all people, including you, are in the image of God. All people should be loved and respected. You should be loved, respected, and honored as one who is created to be like God.

Acknowledgments

I T HAS BEEN three years since I first published *Setting the Captives Free: A Christian Theology of Domestic Violence*. The book has been used in clergy trainings, a seminary class at George Fox Evangelical Seminary, and other abuse-prevention and intervention workshops. However, suggestions for a similar work written for the average reader has challenged me to rethink some of the text. While I feel strongly that *Setting the Captives Free* develops a theology for addressing abuse, the ones who are facilitating change are not concerned with reworking biblical texts and presenting facts, figures, or theology. They want a resource that is easily read, which they can give to churches, to those in abuse, and to those needing support.

In the past three years I have handed the book to many women who were being abused. They are not as concerned about a "Christian theology of domestic violence" as they are about knowing God loves them and wants them to be safe. Abusive men are less inclined to be convinced by the explanation of biblical texts. They need to be held accountable and know that God also wants them to change their behavior.

This book is for them.

Thanks to Wipf and Stock for their constant support in writing and publicizing both books. K. C. Hanson and James Stock have been a great source of encouragement both to me and those who need to read about such a serious and dangerous problem in our churches and communities.

I continue to be amazed at the support from Lori and our sons Nathan, Hunter, and Caleb. While this is not a *Harry Potter* series, they have seemed interested in what I write.

Ron Clark
Agape Church of Christ
Portland, Oregon
www.agapecoc.com

Introduction

Is Domestic Violence a Problem?

SOME PEOPLE TRY to tell me that domestic violence isn't a big problem in their congregation or community. The facts don't bear that out.

- In America two to four million women have indicated that their spouses or live-in partners physically abused them during the year.[1]

- 20 to 25 percent of all women reported that their partners abused them at least once.[2] One out of four American women reports having been raped or physically assaulted by a current or former spouse, by a live-in partner, or by a date at some time in their life.[3]

- 20 to 40 percent of dating couples experience physical violence.[4]

- Hospital emergency rooms indicate that 20 to 30 percent of women seeking treatment are victims of battering.[5]

- Every day in America at least three women are murdered by their husbands or intimate partners.[6]

- Throughout the world, one in three women has confessed to having been beaten, coerced into sex, or has experienced other forms of abuse.[7]

1. Statistics vary, but each year the range of reported cases of abuse falls between 2 and 4 million; see Tjaden and Thoennes, *Full Report of the Prevalence, Incidence, and Consequences of Intimate Partner Violence against Women*; Bancroft, *Why Does He Do That?* 7.

2. Stark and Flitcraft, "Spouse Abuse."

3. Heise, et al., "Ending Violence against Women," 4. See also Levine, "The Perils of Young Romance," 46; National Women's Health Information Center.

4. Hamby, "Acts of Psychological Aggression," 968.

5. Miller, *No Visible Wounds*, 7.

6. Rennison, *Intimate Partner Violence from 1993 to 2001*. In 2000, 1,247 women were killed, while 440 men were killed, by intimate partners. Estrella suggests that every 15 seconds a spouse kills his wife (Estrella, "Effects of Violence on Interpersonal Relations").

7. Heise, et al., "Ending Violence against Women." Estrella reports that 50 percent of women of the world are abused by a spouse, and that 4 million women are involved in sexual trafficking. The statistics vary from country to country. Estrella indicates that 20.8 percent of women in the

- Domestic violence is estimated to be much higher within the United States military than within civilian families.[8]

Domestic violence is an ongoing problem in the United States and throughout the world. This problem not only affects the spouse whom the abuser targets, but it also affects the children in the home.

- One-third of abused women indicate that they were abused the first time during pregnancy.[9] Research suggests that this may contribute to low birth weight of infants and other negative effects for infants.[10]

- In a study done by Boston Medical Center, over one-third of children reported seeing violence by fathers against mothers when a parent reported that no violence occurred.[11]

- Children brought up in abusive homes have a higher risk of being abused.[12]

- It is estimated that five million children per year witness an assault on their mothers.[13]

- "Around forty percent of abusive men extend their behavior pattern to other family members."[14]

These statistics do not include emotional, verbal, and other forms of abuse. Men commit 85 to 90 percent of the reported abuse.[15] The remaining 10 to 15 percent of cases involve women abusing their male intimate partners, and intimate-partner violence between gay and lesbian couples. Thus, it is clear that men are overwhelmingly the cause of pain and suffering on others.

These statistics, however, are only the reported cases. Most abuse goes unreported. Most abuse is hidden from outsiders. Most victims who attend

---

Dominican Republic report having been physically abused, while Palacios reports that in El Salvador four out of five women live with violence in their families (Estrella, "Effects of Violence on Interpersonal Relations and Strategies That Promote Family Unity"; see also Palacios, "Strategies for Working with Latinos Who Have Experienced Family Violence").

8. Hansen, "A Considerate Service," 4; Szegedy-Maszak, "Death at Fort Bragg," 44.

9. Campbell, "Correlates of Battering during Pregnancy," 219–26; Campbell et al, "Why Battering during Pregnancy?" 343–49. As many as 324,000 women each year experience intimate-partner violence during pregnancy. Gazmararian, Petersen, et al., "Violence and Reproductive Health," 79–84.

10. Adams, *Woman-Battering*, 12.

11. Boston Medical Center Pediatrics, "Child Witness to Violence Project."

12. Talbot, "Children Witnessing Domestic Violence."

13. Bancroft, *Why Does He Do That?* 8.

14. Bancroft, *When Dad Hurts Mom*, 53.

15. Rennison and Welchans, *Intimate Partner Violence*, 1.

church keep silent as well. Ministers should be talking about abuse so that victims can feel safe disclosing their experiences of abuse both inside and outside the church. Abuse should be talked about in churches because, as statistics show, some of our men are abusing women. I would suggest that any minister who preaches about abuse will probably have the greatest outreach program any church has known. Abuse is a topic that will impact *at least half* of a congregation.

I have been frustrated with colleagues who feel that raising the topic of abuse is not worth their time. One of my neighbors, an elder of a church, came to an abuse-intervention and prevention training we conducted and invited his minister to attend the next training. This minister told him, "It's not a problem here." When my neighbor shared his minister's remark with me, I suggested to him that within a month someone from his church would come forward about abuse. Three days later he told me of a church member's neighbor who was being abused. The abused church member and her neighbor went to the minister, and he asked not to be involved. My neighbor was frustrated to realize that while his eyes were open, his pastor's were not. It is a shame that someone close to us has to be beaten before we decide that it is a problem.

Domestic violence is not only a crime against humanity; it is a sin against God.

> Open your mouth for those who cannot speak to bring justice to the weak;
>
> Open your mouth and judge righteously, and bring justice to the oppressed and poor. (Prov 31:8–9)[16]

The faith community is called to represent God, to protect victims, and to call men and women to love, compassion, gentleness, and respect for themselves and one another. The community of faith must deal with domestic violence because it has infected our families, our neighborhoods, our community, our churches, and our world. Domestic violence crosses all racial, ethnic, cultural, social, and gender boundaries and is destroying families, children, businesses, friendships, and the structure of our society. Yet a greater crime exists. It is the crime of apathy and silence. To ignore this violence and humiliation is to ignore the voice of God. To pat the victims on the head and minimize their pain is to slap God in the face. To go to our homes and sleep at night, without being compelled to act, while others live in terror is ignoring our duty to God and our neighbor.

---

16. All biblical quotations are my translations. All Hebrew texts are taken from *Biblia Hebraica Stuttgartensia*. All Greek texts are taken from Nestle, et al., *Novum Testamentum Graece*.

It is striking to realize that our government spends millions of dollars to stop terrorism, yet it largely ignores the "domestic terrorism" that occurs every day in homes. Abuse is a problem that needs to be understood and addressed. The abused are humans made in the image of God who need to be protected, loved, and empowered to stand with us and walk through life with respect and dignity. When God brings a victim to us, we have a responsibility to love her as we want to be loved, and to be faithful to this responsibility. We must make sure that victims and their children are safe, protected, and given the chance to live in peace and love. Abusers are also humans made in the image of God, and they need to be taught how to live and respect all others. They must be confronted and challenged to change or face prosecution by our legal system and correction from our spiritual communities.

The faith community is in a great position to address this problem. We have a God who grieves over the violence that occurs in families and over the fact that spiritual leaders have failed the oppressed.

> Hi Ron,
>
> My name is Mary and I'm the director/advocate for Advocate Services which is a crisis center working with victims of domestic violence, sexual assault, elder abuse and child abuse. One of the Portland advocates gave me your address and said that you might have some ideas that will help me with working with the pastors in our area.
>
> #1. The pastors will not return any of my phone calls; rather I call for information or need assistance.
>
> #2. In the past I had three clients return to their abusive homes because the batterer suddenly became religious, and they ended up getting marriage counseling. Of course restraining orders were dropped, etc. Then this past week I moved a domestic violence victim into another small neighboring town so that she could have some peace of mind, and one Pastor called another Pastor and they tracked her down and confronted her on her front lawn at 8:30 pm. Her interpretation of the contact was that she was a bad wife for leaving her husband, she should receive marriage counseling to work it out, and that her husband has been going to church so he's sorry for what he did. Needless to say I had a very long crisis call to this client's residence after they left.
>
> I relish the fact that some of my clients consider the church to be like family and they have these resources to help them through the hard times ahead. But this client states that she will not go back to the church and now she's not only dealing with the loss of a husband who was never there, but also a loss of faith which to me is worse. How do I bridge a gap that I'm not allowed to cross? I know that our Pastors mean well but they do not understand the dynamics behind DV. The women are the ones that suffer in our area. We have had clients kicked out of the congregation until they went back to their husbands.

I'm truly at a loss. We look for any resources that a victim has to help us through the process, and the faith community is slowly becoming more of a hindrance than a resource.

Any ideas of help would be greatly appreciated.[17]

This e-mail from an abuse-intervention advocate illustrates the frustration she has with both the faith community and its leaders. Notice her statements:

- " . . . but also a loss of faith which to me is worse."

- ". . . and the faith community is slowly becoming more of a hindrance than a resource."

- "We have had clients kicked out of the congregation until they went back to their husbands."

The literature on church growth suggests that our American society views the church as irrelevant. The e-mail above confirms why this is true. In this case the advocate claims that the church is a hindrance, and from my experience she is correct. However, by addressing abuse in our churches, we can become powerful allies in God's kingdom.

The rest of this book is an appeal for you to gain an understanding of what it really means to face domestic violence, and how to help bring peace and wholeness to victims and their children caught in the web of abuse. This book is an appeal that you confront those who abuse others and not shut your eyes to the reality of abuse.

17. E-mail to the author in April 2003.

CHAPTER 1

What Is Domestic
Violence?

WHENEVER I SPEAK to groups on the subject of abuse, it is important to begin by defining the terms. People approach this discussion from various backgrounds, contexts, and experiences. The terms used for individuals that are caught in the cycle of violence and abuse will be as follows:

- Those who perpetrate the violence and abuse will be referred to as *abusers*.

- Since the majority of abuse is perpetrated by males against females, the abuser in this book will usually be referred to as male.

- Those who are the recipients of the intimate-partner violence will be referred to as *victims* and usually as female. This is not an attempt to suggest that women are always victims or that men cannot be victims, but *victim* as female is a term with which most readers are familiar.

- While children may also be victims, the focus will be on intimate-partner violence. The children will be separated from *victim* terminology and will be referred to as *children*.

- Child abuse is a sin and a dangerous issue in our society, but the focus of this book is on intimate-partner violence.

- *Family* will be defined as those who are not part of the nuclear family but are related to victims or abusers.

Definition of Abuse

The Oregon Domestic Violence Council has given a good definition of *abuse* that will be used as a model for this discussion. Abuse is:

> A pattern of coercive behavior used by one person to control and subordinate another in an intimate relationship. These behaviors include physical, sexual, psychological, and economic abuse. Tactics of

coercion, terrorism, degradation, exploitation, and violence are used to engender fear in the victim in order to enforce compliance.[1]

Three key points in this definition will be discussed more fully. First, the definition uses the term *coercive behavior*. This suggests manipulation of another person to get what one desires. The definition mentions that the goal of the abuser is to enforce compliance. *Coercion* suggests control and an expression of power over another person. This coercion and control can occur through the use of threats, violence, humiliation, exploitation, or even self-pity. *Abuse* is not about anger; it is about control and forced compliance.

In order to understand how power and control interact in an abusive relationship, let us look at the Power and Control Wheel in figure 1. This diagram was created by the Domestic Abuse Intervention Project in Duluth, Minnesota, and has become a standard diagram used in domestic-violence training.

Figure 1: Abuse Power and Control Wheel. Copied with Permission, Domestic Abuse Intervention Project: 202 East Superior Street, Duluth, MN 55802.

1. Multnomah County Health Department et al., *Domestic Violence in Multnomah County*, 3.

The wheel in figure 1 indicates that the hub of abuse is *power and control.* Abusers focus on controlling and displaying power over others. They do not always use physical violence. They use whatever they must in order to enforce compliance. These abusers may intimidate and threaten their victims. If these tactics do not work, then they will try something else. Their goal is to gain control of others.

> The aim of all abuse, unlike that of sadism, is not the pleasure of inflicting pain, but the need to control: domination is the end in itself. While a man may explain his actions by saying, "I lost control," in fact what he did was *gain* control.[2]

The spokes of the wheel (figure 1) separate the different types of control that abusers may use. Abusers use various tactics to force compliance in another person. They may use threats, intimidation, or male privilege; they may withhold finances and isolate their partners. In situations where they have children, the kids are manipulated to keep the abused partner in compliance. Patricia Evans illustrates two realities of the abusive relationship and the imbalance that exists (figure 2).[3] The realities of the abuser suggest that the world of the abuser is one of selfishness and control rather than love and compassion.

What is present in the relationship is:	What is lacking in the relationship is:
Inequality	Equality
Competition	Partnership
	Mutuality
Hostility	Goodwill
Control	Intimacy
Negation	Validation

Figure 2: The Reality of the World of the Abuser

We tend to view abusers as angry people who are out of control. They use whatever tactics necessary to gain control over others.

> The emotionally abusive person has an agenda, and that agenda is to be in control. In his attempt to be in control he will dominate, suppress, tyrannize, persecute, and attempt to conquer anyone he relates to on a consistent basis. Among his repertoire of control tactics are insults, denigrating comments, derogatory words, threats, and constant

2. Miller, *No Visible Wounds,* 17.
3. Evans, *The Verbally Abusive Relationship,* 42.

criticism, along with an extensive array of other intimidating behavior designed to make others feel inadequate and helpless.[4]

The goal of abusers is control.[5] Abusers can also use apologies, self-pity, and sympathy to control a situation.

This is an example of *coercion*. When abusers want to have their own way, they will use anger, apology, instruction, and anything else available to *prove their point of view* or *enforce compliance*. This control is grounded in an unwillingness to admit wrong and take the necessary steps to change *their* behavior. It is also grounded in a narcissistic attitude, which will be discussed further in a later chapter. Narcissism is a preoccupation or infatuation with oneself. For abusers, the issue is not about changing themselves but about coercing others to change or accept their behavior. Abusers do not feel that they are wrong; they believe that they are misunderstood and need to help others understand and approve of their actions! They seek to control others' perception about their behavior.

"I didn't mean to hurt her," he said.

"But you did," I replied.

"It's just, it's just that I want her to understand me," he slowly muttered.

"What do you mean, 'understand you'?"

"When I get mad and cuss at her, she just leaves and won't let me explain. That's why I grab her and try to talk to her, but she won't listen."

"Why don't you just let her walk away? Isn't it better to let her go and cool off and then talk to her later?" I asked.

"She might not come back and I don't want her to think that that is how I am," he said.

"So it is OK for you to use violence to make her understand?" I asked.

"No, but I try to tell her that those actions are not me," he responded.

"What do you mean, not you? Is someone else doing this?"

"Well, it's not me; I mean it is, but it is a part of me I need to shove down—it's a bad part that I am trying to control," he said. "When she doesn't listen, the bad comes out and I just can't stop it. I tell her that, but sometimes she makes it worse."

"Steve, Jesus says that you will know them by their fruits. I believe that we do what we choose to do. This is who you are, and it is not about Karen understanding you; it is about you changing your behavior. Grabbing another person

4. Engel, *The Emotionally Abused Woman*, 47.
5. Bancroft, *Why Does He Do That?* 112.

so hard that they bruise is wrong, especially when they want to walk away and cool off."

"But she bruises easy," he said.

"I don't buy that," I responded.

"Then how do I make her understand me?"

"You don't," I said. "You start by trying to understand yourself."

The second key point in the Oregon Domestic Violence Council's definition is, "to control and subordinate another . . . to engender fear."[6] This suggests an unequal relationship between two human beings. "The term *abuse* is about *power*, it means that a person is taking advantage of a power imbalance to exploit or control someone else."[7] People are meant to live together in harmony and equality, not fear. The marriage/dating relationship does not change this basic human right. No one has the privilege, from God or anyone else, to *control* or *subordinate* another person. No one has the right to cause fear in a relationship. We do not accept this in our friendships, and we should not accept it in our intimate relationships. Abusive relationships do not involve shared power. These relationships are foreign to God's method of relationship.

Finally the council's definition states that the victim is in "an intimate relationship" with the abuser. This intimacy creates a strong bond between the abuser and the victim and is difficult to break. This produces a dangerous interplay of emotion and passion expressed by the abuser, who is trying to control both his environment and his partner. This interplay then causes the abuse to become cyclical. "It seems absurd that a relationship that is supposed to be based on love can become violent and demeaning. The incredulity is stretched even further when the relationship does not dissolve but instead continues in a cycle of apparent forgiveness and sentimental love followed by increased violence."[8]

Our family is a fan of the reality show *The Amazing Race*. We often comment how intense the conflict seems to be among couples who are in an intimate relationship. Those who are friends or have parent-child relationships generally seem to handle the stress and frustration with little verbal abuse and criticism. Yet some of the married, dating, or formerly intimate couples use harsh criticism and abusive language toward each other. It does seem interesting that in this show couples in intimate relationships seem to be more abusive

6. Multnomah County Health Department et al., *Domestic Violence in Multnomah County*, 3.

7. Bancroft, *Why Does He Do That?* 123.

8. Livingston, *Healing Violent Men*, 7.

in their treatment of each other. The stress of the race continually intensifies the abusive tendencies and behavior among these couples. Somehow the abusive personality believes that the intimate relationship gives them *entitlement* to control their partner.

Abuse continues not only because the abuser is controlling the victim, but also because the victim feels loved by the abuser and feels a sense of duty to stay in the relationship to keep the family together. Sometimes the good memories of their intimacy can override the painful memories.

> While those who emotionally abuse others don't always intend to destroy those around them, they do set out to control them. And what better way to control someone than to make her doubt her perceptions? What better way than to cause her to have such low self-esteem that she becomes dependent on her abuser? Emotional-abuse victims become so convinced they are worthless that they believe no one else could possible want them. Therefore, they stay in abusive situations because they believe they have nowhere else to go. Their ultimate fear is that of being all alone.[9]

If the couple has children, sometimes the fear of being a single parent causes the victim to continue in the relationship.[10]

> Society has long instilled the idea that unless children are raised by two parents . . . they will grow up somehow warped; as a result mothers often suffer prolonged abuse for what they explain as "the good of my children." . . .
>
> The truth is that it is far better to have no father than to have a destructive one, because as psychiatrists have found, one nurturing parent is sufficient to foster a child's healthy development. A child who grows up hearing his father's constant put-downs of his mother, who absorbs his father's manipulative skills like osmosis through his pores, who models his father's macho domination and watches his mother submit in fear—this child cannot grow up whole. He will instead grow up twisted by the dread he felt, guilty over his inability to protect his mother, and angry that, too small and helpless, he couldn't cry out.[11]

Many women choose to stay in the relationship out of fear. One thing must be understood: the victim is not choosing the abuse; they are trying

---

9. Engel, *The Emotionally Abused Woman*, 11.

10. Amato and Booth, "Consequences of Parental Divorce and Marital Unhappiness for Adult Well-Being," 895–914; and Garbardi, and Rosen, "Intimate Relationships," 25–26. Children are actually much more susceptible to dysfunctional behaviors if they live in dysfunctional and violent homes.

11. Miller, *No Visible Wounds*, 137–38.

to strengthen or stay in the relationship. Other times victims are taught that they can change the abuser through submitting to him, loving him more, or making him happy. I have had many women confess to me that their ministers counseled them to stay and take this attitude. However, the abuser has to choose to change himself.

Abuse Is Cyclical

Abuse is *cyclical*. Abuse usually is not a one-time event. Figure 3 illustrates how this cyclical relationship can progress through three phases. There is tension, which can develop into a violent storm, followed by the cam after the storm. This cycle occurs because the *abuser* is not able to effectively address his anxiety.

Calm After the Storm

Storm

Tension

Figure 3: Cycle of Abuse

An abuser may explode, be bitter, or become aggressive, but the test is how he expresses his anger. Is anger used to control, intimidate, coerce, or manipulate others? Can he switch from anger to sympathy and still attempt to "win"? An abuser may not use anger (especially if he knows it will not work in a situation) but may use different emotions to control and coerce others.

> One of the earliest lessons I learned from abused women is that to understand abuse you can't look just at the explosions, you have to examine with equal care the spaces *between* the explosions. The dynamics of these periods tell us as much about the abuse as the rages or the thrown objects, as the disgusting name-calling or the jealous accusations. The abuser's thinking and behavior during the calmer periods are what cause his big eruptions that wound or frighten.[12]

12. Bancroft, *Why Does He Do That?* 137–38.

Abusers many times feel they are in control of their emotions and surroundings. While abusers may suggest that they are in control of the situation, the opposite actually happens. They are losing control over others, since people and human behavior are not always predictable, and this unpredictability brings about fear and a desire to achieve more control.

One phase of this cycle is the *tension phase*. During this phase the abuser may display higher amounts of anxiety and emotion. Pressures from work, sleep deprivation, or other events may increase his level of anxiety. The abuser becomes edgy and critical around those with whom he has an intimate relationship. The victim or children become scapegoats of the abuser's problems and are made to feel responsible for the abuser's behavior. The victim can usually sense this phase and predict its intensity. Some call it the "walking-on-eggshells phase." Tension builds, and the abuser acts out as a result of his anxiety. This generally is the time when a victim will reach out to others, knowing that the storm is about to erupt. The victim tries to avoid making the abuser angry, hoping that the storm will pass. The family revolves around the anxiety level of the abuser. One woman told me, "When he came home smiling, we all breathed a sigh of relief. When he came home angry, we were on edge."

The next phase of the cycle is the *storm phase*. At this point, the abuser uses whatever is at his disposal to control others. This may be the point when the husband first cusses out his wife, or when the wife degrades her husband. The abuse escalates. It may develop into physical violence, depending on the behavior of the abuser or the intensity of the cycle. For some, it takes years before physical abuse happens; for others, it happens immediately. Having counseled women and men in abuse, I have seen this pattern occurring at various levels of intensity. It doesn't matter what the victim has done to try to avoid the storm; it comes, and there is little to stop it. An outside source may bring temporary relief and silence the storm for a time, but the tension will return and the storm will happen. In this phase the abuser acts out by hurting those around him.

The third phase is the *calm after the storm*. During this phase the abuser feels sorry, guilty, or ashamed. He verbally repents, makes promises, gives gifts, or weeps with the victim. He does not seem to be an angry person, but he still attempts to control the victim. He fears that the victim will leave and not return, so he promises to change his behavior. He worries about how this looks to others. He can be kind, sweet, charming, and even romantic. He uses coercion and control to "keep the family together," not realizing that he is acting out of fear and selfishness. He will offer to go to counseling, but it is usually only a concession. He may deny the event happened or minimize the abuse. The victim who asked for help during the tension phase now feels that everything is better, and that they were exaggerating the situation. Children many times are conceived during this period. Commitments are made in the religious community, counseling sessions are started, and sometimes new things are bought for the family. As with any storm, the scars and damage are still visible. The calm is temporary. Sadly though, the victim sees the cycle begin again. Yet this time there are more responsibilities and attachments as a result of the calm after the storm phase. The abuser has not changed, but he has coerced his partner to invest more into the relationship, which makes it that much harder to leave. The abuser reminds the victim that she could have avoided the storm. Each time the cycle repeats, the storm is more violent and the honeymoon period becomes shorter.

Abuse Can Escalate

Abuse is *likely to continue or escalate unless there is intervention*. When the calm passes, the abuser's attempt to control intensifies. The abuser is narcissistic, which means that he is focused on his own needs and emotions. This attitude causes the victim to be in danger if she leaves, and if she returns he will remind her that he is in power.[13] The two most dangerous times in an abused woman's life happen when she leaves, and when she becomes pregnant. The abuser feels that his needs must be met. The abuser also feels that he almost lost his partner but has now increased the investment in the relationship through gifts, commitments, and promises. The abuser continues to control but may introduce new methods of coercion into the relationship. He may say that the victim made him angry and may give subtle reminders concerning the "night of the storm." This again is an attempt to intimidate and warn the victim not "to cross me again." A raised hand, a fist, or a threat will remind the victim that the storm can come at any time. Depending on the intensity of the relationship and abuse, the transition from the calm-after-the-storm phase to the tension phase can range from a few days to years. It may repeat, only with more intensity. The abuse cycle can escalate like a violent storm or tornado and can subside quickly. "Abuse never—and I use the word *never* fully aware of its pitfalls—goes away of its own accord; it escalates. Name-calling grows into public humiliation, isolation, and eventually threats, at which level a union may continue until death do them part; on the other hand, threats may become the reality of beatings and murder."[14] The abuser acts as if he controls

13. Burch and Gallup, "Pregnancy as a Stimulus for Domestic Violence," 246; and Martin, et al., "Changes in Intimate Partner Violence during Pregnancy," 201–10.

14. Miller, *No Visible Wounds*, 10.

the weather, and the victim determines the type of weather. Unfortunately victims of abuse are traumatized, as are storm victims. Those who have lived through tornados or hurricanes are emotionally and physically affected.

The best way to break this cycle is through intervention. Someone has to break the cycle and stop the escalating danger. Sometimes the police arrest the abuser and the cycle ends for a brief period of time. Other times the victim leaves; however, the abuser is more likely to kill his victim if she leaves home for a time. "The abusive man becomes more dangerous when he loses all contact with his partner. There is a sense of urgency for a man when he feels out of control or abandoned. He may even experience this abandonment as a threat to his very existence, so that he feels that regaining control or reestablishing the relationship is a matter of life or death."[15]

The abuser feels abandoned by his spouse or partner and may violently pursue her, not because of a sense of remorse but because of a need for control. Statistics show that a married woman who leaves an abusive relationship is in greater danger of being murdered than those who are dating or cohabiting with their partner. Somehow the abuser sees marriage as his entitlement to "his wife."[16]

Sometimes the family or a community intervenes, protects the victim, and holds the abuser accountable. If the abuser attempts to revive the relationship and is successful, the cycle may restart. If he finds another partner, the cycle can begin again. This cycle will continue until the abuser practices shared power and mutual respect with the partner. If the relationship continues, the abuser must change his behavior in order for the cycle to end. The abuser is responsible for the cycle, not the victim. "As long as we see abusers as victims or as out-of-control monsters, they will continue getting away with ruining lives. If we want abusers to change, we will have to require them to give up the luxury of exploitation."[17]

In interviews with victims, I have found that some try to display their own sense of control in order to survive in the abusive relationship. Victims have taken beatings for their children or parents. Some have found the tension phase so stressful that they have challenged the abuser in order to get past the storm. One woman shared that her mother was coming to visit in two weeks, so she felt that it was better to get a black eye now so that it would heal before her mother arrived. Some found that they could occasionally avoid the storm

15. Livingston, *Healing Violent Men*, 22.

16. The victim's greatest danger happens in the first few weeks after she leaves her abuser. Victimization rates in married women separated from their abuser are three times higher than those divorced from an abuser (Clements et al., "Dysphoria and Hopelessness Following Battering," 25).

17. Bancroft, *Why Does He Do That?* 157.

phase but they also knew that other times there was little they could do to stop it. This attempt at control is dangerous and happens when the victim sees no way out. In some cases counselors or ministers blame the victim as the one "pushing his buttons." This is called "victim blaming." It is not an acceptable method of support. Intervention must occur so that the victim does not have to live with this imbalance of power.

While challenging an abuser and so suffering abuse seems odd to many, it is a typical method of survival. Victims do what they have to do to survive. Victims never should be judged for the reason they have suffered abuse; they should be supported for their desire to survive. Victim blaming further damages those suffering from abuse. Victims should be encouraged to be strong rather than be humiliated for trying to adapt. The cycle of abuse is dangerous and violent, and victims many times feel that they are alone. They have been isolated, intimidated, manipulated, humiliated, and violated. They feel powerless. They have been told that the abuse is their fault. They need to be validated. They need to be strengthened to stand, with the rest of the community, and to call the abuser to accountability. They need to know that they can remove themselves from the cycle of abuse and find safety.

Domestic violence involves coercion, control, subordination, and an intimate relationship. The goal of the abuser is to enforce compliance and engender fear. The cycle of abuse continues because the abuser enjoys the benefits of this cycle. This is destructive to the spiritual development of others. Healthy relationships are grounded in love, respect, and encouragement. God empowers people to make their own choices and gives free will. Church leaders, counselors, and friends are to encourage others to be the best they can be.

Types of Abuse

Abuse can take many forms; therefore, definitions of *abuse* may differ. The list that follows is not exhaustive, but it introduces the main types of abuse.

Physical Abuse

We are most commonly aware of *physical abuse*. This is usually the type the media displays. Physical abuse involves any form of physical action used to control another person. The most obvious forms are hitting, punching, slapping, kicking, shoving, choking, pulling hair or other body parts, and throwing objects at another person.[18] These forms of physical abuse involve abusers

18. Dugan and Hock, *It's My Life Now*, 6; Miles, *Domestic Violence*, 111–13; and Weitzman, *"Not to People Like Us,"* 88.

directly attacking the victims in an attempt to punish them or control their actions. To perpetrate physical abuse is to invade the victim's personal space. Physical abuse may leave bruises, marks, or other, invisible signs of trauma. "Your partner may have hit you hard enough to leave bruises, but he was careful to hit you only on parts of your body where others would not see them. He may have grabbed you and twisted your arm sufficiently to cause real pain, but he didn't leave a noticeable mark. If he threw you against a wall or pushed you to the floor, no one else would have known."[19]

Forms of physical abuse that may not be as obvious are grabbing or restraining another person by the hair or body parts, and forcing another to stop their movement. These are not as obvious to outsiders because they usually do not leave bruises or marks and can be interpreted by the abuser or victim as roughhousing or simply as a warning. The abuser may also suggest that if he had wanted to hurt the other person, then he would have used a direct attack. The abuser may tell the victim that he didn't mean to act so roughly. These forms of physical abuse also force victims to change behavior or to use a physical response themselves. An example of this occurs when an abuser blocks the door so that a victim cannot leave. The victim is forced to stay where she is, or to physically attempt to move the abuser. This is still physical abuse because it is an attempt by the abuser to intimidate, control, or coerce the other person. It is also a violation of and unwelcome entry into a person's physical space.

Verbal or Emotional Abuse

While physical abuse is the most obvious type of abuse, verbal and emotional abuse is the most common. Very few people feel confident reporting this type of abuse because they assume that the abuser is only "losing his temper" or "not thinking before he talks." While at times this may be true, abuse begins when negative words control another person. Verbal and emotional abuse is usually a direct attack on the individual. The abuser uses words and emotions to humiliate or shame the other person. Abusers may resort to name-calling; threatening the other person's emotions or personal items; yelling; insulting; blaming; disregarding the other person's feelings; criticizing the other person's language skills, culture, or physical appearance; or harming a pet.[20] This direct

---

19. Dugan and Hock, *It's My Life Now*, 5–6.

20. Awareness has increased of a correlation between animal abuse and domestic violence. Veterinary conferences have included sessions about domestic violence in families and the effects on animals. Abusers may injure or kill a family pet in order to cause fear in or control the rest of the family (Miles, *Domestic Violence*, 112).

abuse causes the other person to feel guilty, ashamed, afraid, and humiliated, and it encourages the other person to be silent: "As with physical violence, verbal abuse can take many different forms, but the result is to change your view of yourself."[21] "Emotional battering, then, runs the gamut from a steady grinding down of a woman to emotional trauma. While her bones are never broken, her flesh never bruised, her blood never spilled, she is wounded nonetheless. With self-confidence and self-respect gone, she lives, empty, with no self left to assert. She cedes control of her life to her abuser. She is helpless."[22]

Grace Ketterman writes that verbal abuse is more damaging to the soul of victims than physical abuse. She believes that *verbal abuse precedes other forms of abuse and neglect and also affects a person's self-esteem.*[23] Patricia Evans also suggests that verbal abuse affects an individual's personal view of life:

> Verbal abuse is damaging to the spirit. It takes the joy and vitality out of life. It distorts reality because the abuser's response does not correlate with the partner's communication. The partner usually believes the abuser is being honest and straightforward with her and has some reason for what he says—if only she could figure out what it is. When the abuser's response does not correlate with her communications to him, the partner usually tries again to express herself more adequately so he will understand her.[24]

According to Ketterman, verbal abuse has seven different ingredients.[25]

- Verbal abuse causes *emotional damage* because of the victim's sense of *rejection* of their value as a person.

- Verbal abuse may *isolate* a person from friendships by *destroying* the self-esteem needed for these relationships.

- Verbal abuse *creates terror* in the victim.

- Verbal abuse *ignores* the victim's basic needs.

- Verbal abuse *corrupts* the values and behaviors of the victim.

- Verbal abuse *degrades* the victim by robbing the person of self-esteem.

- Verbal abuse *exploits* the victim to the benefit of the abuser.

21. Ibid., 6.

22. Miller, *No Visible Wounds*, 32.

23. Ketterman, *Verbal Abuse*, 13.

24. Evans, *The Verbally Abusive Relationship*, 50–51.

25. Ketterman, *Verbal Abuse*, 12–13. Evans also has a quite-exhaustive list of consequences and affects of verbal abuse on the victim (Evans, *The Verbally Abusive Relationship*, 50).

Physical bruises may heal in a few days, but emotional bruises can last a lifetime. Verbal abuse is designed to humiliate, control, and cause self-doubt in the partner. One victim told me that the bruises healed, but the words burned in her mind. Whoever said, "Sticks and stones may break my bones but words will never hurt me," was wrong![26]

Indirectly one may use verbal and emotional abuse to evoke a response or change in the other person. Abusers may threaten to injure or kill themselves, friends, or relatives. They may badger, beg, plead, or harass their partner into consenting to their wishes. They may tell the victim, "You're not really hurt; suck it up." They may withhold information or affection from the victim. The abuser can turn the abuse inward in order to cause the victim to feel sorry and apologize for her actions. "You made me do this" or "Can't you see what you have done to me?" are examples of verbal and emotional abuse, which attempt to take the focus off the victim's feelings and onto the abuser's. This keeps the abuse cyclical and moves the relationship from the honeymoon phase to the tension phase. "After each incident of abuse, your partner probably tried to make it seem as though you caused it. It may have gone something like, 'I'm so sorry but if only you hadn't . . .' This created a way to seem repentant while telling you it was really all your fault."[27]

This *indirect* form of verbal and emotional abuse causes the other person to be confused, and lowers her self-esteem and her trust in herself. "The emotionally abused woman is a particular type of woman, a woman who has established a pattern of continually being emotionally abused by those she is involved with, whether it be her lover or husband, her boss, her friends, her parents, her children, or her siblings. No matter how successful, how intelligent, or how attractive she is, she still feels 'less than' other people."[28]

Sexual Abuse

Coercion of sexual activity with another person with or without the other's consent is rape. When the abuser expects, forces, or initiates unwanted sexual contact with the other person, it is abuse. A relationship between two people does not give one a right to force or manipulate another into having sex. Although sex is meant to be an enjoyable experience, an abuser may try to

---

26. "The resilient body mends with ointments and splints—physically battered women know that in their pain. But so deep is the wounding of emotional battering, so down-reaching the anguish, so hopeless the mending that, as the Spanish maxim says, 'He that loseth his spirit loseth all.' The emotionally battered woman loses herself" (Miller, *No Visible Wounds*, 32).

27. Dugan and Hock, *It's My Life Now*, 8.

28. Engel, *The Emotionally Abused Woman*, 7.

control the experience of pleasure in the other person. Sex will either be enjoyable only for the abuser or will be a form of punishment of or control over the victim. The victim usually feels humiliation, shame, and guilt when this type of abuse happens.

Sexual abuse can also happen *indirectly*. Whenever a person, organization, or community manipulates others into consenting to have sex with another, it is abuse. Abuse may involve badgering, coercing, or verbally assaulting another person into consenting to have sex; engaging in prostitution; or spouse swapping. While the victim may have "willingly consented" to sexual contact, this is still a form of coercion and manipulation. The abuser may also manipulate others to coerce the victim through religious teachings, cultural values, humiliation, money, bartering, or marital roles to consent to sexual contact. Spouses coerced into spouse swapping are also victims. In the case of spouse swapping, victims feel confusion, shame, and guilt, because they are convinced that they chose this action.

Two shelters contacted me to mediate an issue between Robert and Cecilia. Cecilia was at the women's homeless shelter and Robert was at the men's shelter. She had filed abuse charges against him and had filed for divorce after Robert was convicted. The two shelters were in disagreement over how to handle the situation. The women felt a need to empower Cecilia, and the men felt the same for Robert. Yet the men felt that Cecilia was not acting within God's will when she filed for divorce.

After meeting with the counselors of each shelter, I found that the men knew of Robert's abuse conviction and were holding him accountable. Cecilia had told the women counselors that Robert was still harassing her and threatening her over the telephone. Since they were staying in different shelters, he was not able to see her, but he still found ways to talk to her. Robert's counselors, unaware of his telephone calls, felt he was coming along and were trying to arrange conjugal visits between Robert and Cecilia. Cecilia and her counselors were uncomfortable with this. The men counselors had a difficult time understanding why this was uncomfortable for Cecilia. This frustrated the women counselors—hence the need for mediation. Cecilia was placed in a vulnerable position controlled by Robert. He was controlling the counselors who, in turn, were using the Bible to coerce Cecilia into further victimization. The use of Scripture and "theology" to coerce her into sex was an example of direct and indirect sexual abuse by all the men involved.

God created humans male and female to share a sexual relationship out of love, respect, and compassion. In the biblical book of Proverbs, Agur tells us that the way of a man with a maiden is wonderful (Prov 30:18–19). This is how a sexual relationship is meant to be—with shared power and respect!

Neglect

Another common form of abuse is *neglect*. Current research suggests that neglect and poor parenting (antisocial behavior) are powerful indicators that children may repeat abuse in adulthood.[29] Neglect is defined as behavior that withholds emotional satisfaction or physical necessities. An abuser may withhold food, liquids, clothing, protection, emotional support, verbal communication, finances, or anything else the other person needs for survival.[30] Abusers may fail to properly guide, develop, and nurture their children due to their own selfishness. They may also isolate family members physically, emotionally, and geographically in order to prevent them from developing relationships with others. The victim will feel abandoned and unloved as a result of this neglect.

Indirectly abusers may also manipulate victims into sacrificing their personal needs and desires for the sake of the abuser or for others. Through coercion and control, abusers evoke sacrifice and giving from the victim for their own benefit. They may try to manipulate clergy into suggesting that their wives "serve" more. While this form of abuse is hard to see, it is common among spiritual communities and families that may appear deeply religious. While the victim may feel a sense of worth by giving, it is second to the sense of satisfaction and control that the abuser experiences.

> The impact of severe neglect on persons is as damaging as acts that are more intentionally and actively perpetrated. In addition, the worst forms of human-induced trauma are those in which some violent act against a person is followed by a period of neglect and lack of support.[31]

29. "Although witnessing family violence uniquely contributed to prediction of psychological spouse abuse, it was childhood neglect that accounted for the largest amount of unique variance in physical spouse abuse scores." Bevan and Higgins, "Is Domestic Violence Learned?" 239. Simons et al. write that ineffective parenting increases the chance of dating violence in their children rather than modeling or exposure to harsh corporal punishment. "Children are at risk for developing antisocial patterns of behavior when they are exposed to ineffective parenting practices such as low supervision, rejection, and inconsistent discipline." Simons, et al., "Socialization in the Family of Origin and Male Dating Violence," 468–69.

30. While some list financial abuse as a separate category, I feel that the withholding of finances seems to fit better under the definition of neglect.

31. Means, *Trauma & Evil*, 16.

When a man becomes violent, those in the intimate relationship become confused. The refusal to acknowledge wrong and change behavior leaves the victim asking the question, is this really his nature? The abuser must acknowledge that his actions are wrong or sinful and take responsibility for his behavior. Neglect may be an unwillingness to be accountable for one's actions to those who have been wronged.

Secondhand Abuse

Finally I would like to suggest another form of abuse not commonly discussed, *secondhand abuse*. Just as research has shown the harmful effects of secondhand smoke, so research indicates that children who witness acts of domestic violence are harmed in their emotional, mental, and physical development.[32] Children who witness physical abuse between parents are subjected to horrible acts of violence. Children who also witness intense verbal abuse between parents are also affected mentally.[33] Children may be the victims of physical, emotional, verbal, or sexual abuse actually intended for the other adult. Sometimes pregnant victims have lost unborn babies due to a physical blow by the abuser. In Oregon, abusers who use physical violence on their partner in front of a child are given stricter punishment in the legal system due to the realization of the effects of second hand abuse. Children who witness domestic violence suffer from sleep difficulties, somatic complaints, aggressive behavior, attention deficit disorder (ADD), posttraumatic stress disorder (PTSD), and depression.[34] The saying is true, "Little pictures have big ears," and eyes.

Abuse may take many forms, including physical abuse, verbal abuse, emotional abuse, sexual abuse, secondhand abuse, and neglect. While this list is not exhaustive, it gives us a good framework with which to begin. Usually domestic violence involves more than one form of abuse. All may contribute to the dysfunction in an abusive home, as well as to the behaviors and coping skills the family uses to survive. Unfortunately, not all the forms of abuse mentioned here are illegal. While they are all gross violations of human rights, a victim will not likely be able to obtain a restraining order for neglect. Even though our legal system will prosecute someone committing many of these forms of abuse that occur in the home every day without prosecution or

32. Ibid., 223–45; Anderson and Cramer-Benjamin, "The Impact of Couple Violence on Parenting and Children," 1–19; Bancroft, *The Batterer as Parent*, 37–41; and *When Dad Hurts Mom*, 76, 145–46; Jouriles, et al., "Knives, Guns, and Interparent Violence," 178–94; Straton, "What Is Fair for Children of Abusive Men?" 1–10.

33. Straton, "What Is Fair for Children of Abusive Men?" 5.

34. Boston Medical Center Pediatrics, "Child Witness to Violence Project."

conviction. A man can verbally and emotionally abuse his wife in front of a police officer and not be charged with abuse.

Fortunately in faith communities we can communicate that these forms of abuse are sinful and unacceptable for the people of God to practice or to allow to be practiced. God expects the community to respond to the cries of victims.

The Apostle Paul writes that the fruits of the Spirit are love, joy, peace, endurance, compassion, goodness, gentleness, faithfulness, and self-control (Gal 5:22–23). These are opposite the works of the flesh that include violence, selfishness, and hatred (Gal 5:19–21). All communities of faith should clearly teach the practices of love and peace in community as well as in personal relationships. The types of abuse discussed above are contrary to the spirit of the Creator and the God who loves and frees people. In an attempt to reflect the nature of God, faith communities can adopt a zero-tolerance policy for any of these forms of abuse and can encourage shared power in relationships rather than coercion, control, and power over another.

Since abuse involves control and power over another person, we must discuss how abuse controls others. Once we understand how abuse "controls victims, we can help to dispel the myths of abuse that so saturate our understanding of domestic violence. Domestic violence is not about anger or losing control. It is about power and control. Abusers use various types of abuse to control and coerce those with whom they are intimate. Unless this cycle is broken, those who try to exert power and control over others are violating basic human rights as well as spiritual values. Because we are created, male and female, in the image of God, then it should not be in our nature to control others. *Yahweh* is one who empowers people to grow and develop physically, emotionally, and spiritually. Because we bear God's image, we must also empower others through shared power, respect, and love.

The spiritual community must address domestic violence from the perspective of abusive power and control. First, the source of spirituality, God, is not abusive or controlling. Second, the community must reflect our Creator by confronting abusive behavior and empowering victims to be strong and safe. Third, faith communities are to protect victims Instead of further oppressing them or humiliating them, we must empower them to be safe and loved. Too often the faith community calls victims to forgive their abusers rather than calling the abusers or oppressors to repentance.

CHAPTER 2

What Issues Do Those in Abuse Face?

IN THE FIRST chapter we defined some of the terms used to discuss domestic violence. I suggested that abuse originates in a need for power and control rather than in anger and loss of control. Anxiety and stress may intensify power and control issues in an individual, but they are not the source of abuse. An abuser may use physical, sexual, verbal, or emotional abuse, or neglect, to coerce a person into submission. I also suggested that these tactics may be direct or indirect. Intimate-partner violence is cyclical and can escalate when continuing over a long period of time.

Because of the issues of power and control, escalating violence, and various types of abuse, the effects of domestic violence on the family are traumatic. Affected members are caught in an intricate web of deceit, violence, submission, and manipulation. When trying to work with victims, children, or abusers one should understand the family system and how it affects the members. This chapter discusses the issues that victims, abusers, children, and other family members will face while living in an abusive home.

Victims

Most of the victims whom we work with are women. It has been estimated that 85 to 90 percent of abuse happens to women by male intimate partners.[1] Abuse can occur in marriages, cohabitations, and dating relationships. The victims in these relationships face tremendous obstacles trying to survive and find safety. Too often outsiders try to rescue victims. Popular songs and movies on the subject of abuse have the woman killing the abuser, running to a protective lover, or having a friend plot to kill the abuser. This rescuer mentality is based on the assumption that the victim wants to be saved. The victim wants to be safe and respected, but trying to "save" her is to manipulate further. This does not empower the victim to confront the abuser and abuse.

1. Clark, *Setting the Captives Free*, 32–33.

The victim is being taken away from home and placed in another environment, sometimes against her will. This is not what the victim needs.

She told Lori and me that she had been abused in the past. Tammy and Mike had come to me for counseling and both admitted that he had hit her. After further discussion, Tammy told me of an incident where she called the police after Mike had beaten her. The police officer had told Tammy that she was crazy to go back to Mike after what he had done. This caused me to think that Tammy and Mike were minimizing the abuse. After a month Tammy called me from her trailer. Lori and I rushed out to help protect her. She had four children, and they lived in a trailer park about ten miles outside of town. Mike had disconnected the telephone and was planning to move further out in the country. Lori and I spent a half hour at the next-door neighbor's home calling the shelter to see if they had room. They were full but willing to make room. The time was right. Mike was drunk and at a friend's trailer down the road. He had his gun and had been drinking all afternoon.

We spent an hour persuading Tammy to leave with the children. We talked and talked and persuaded with everything we had. The adrenaline was flowing and we were on a roll, not even thinking about what could happen if Mike came home. Would he attack Tammy and/or the kids for informing me about his abuse? Would he actually "shoot the preacher"? Would he consider us the enemy? She finally consented, and then it took her another hour to get ready. Tammy loaded the kids with a few belongings into the old van. They followed us to the shelter and spent the night there. Lori and I went home exhausted but feeling good. We had saved another one.

The next day Tammy called Mike and went back home. From what the shelter worker told me, he told Tammy he had a good stash of marijuana for her and promised not to hit her any more.

What a rollercoaster ride! What a disappointment! What a shame! What manipulation! I am not talking about the husband—I am talking about Lori and me, who obviously *coerced* a woman to leave when that was not what she wanted to do. This is not always the best way to help. We did what we felt we had to do at the time, but helping victims is not about whisking them away on our magic carpets. Helping victims is about empowering them to be strong. When working with victims, it is important to understand what they want for themselves. Studies illustrate that almost 92 percent of abused women surveyed indicate that what they want most from another person is a listening ear.[2] This suggests overwhelmingly that victims want to be heard. The first issue that is important to victims is *validation*.

The people of Israel were comforted when God validated their suffering: "When they heard that *Yahweh* was concerned about them and had seen their misery, they bowed and worshipped" (Exod 4:31). Victims cannot worship or be free until they feel validated. Many times victims are afraid that their confession or experiences will be met with "I can't believe it!" or "Are you sure?" Sharing the painful experience of abuse with others is humiliating, and victims take a great risk when they open up to another person. An abuser has minimized their pain, and victims have been manipulated and confused for so long that they question their own experiences.[3] They have also been taught by the abuser, and many times by unbelieving family members and friends, to ignore the inner voice. Victims need to know that they do not deserve to be mistreated. Above all else, when others hear a victim's story, listeners should say, "I believe you," "I want to listen," or "I am sorry that this is happening to you."

> The traditional view of psychotherapy holds that once you sort out your inner conflicts, your behavior will change. Insight precedes action. But when it comes to the abused upscale wife, I have found that outsight— the validation that others bring from the outside by concretizing the experience with words and recognition—precedes insight, which in turn precedes action. Validation must occur before the woman will recognize what is happening and take action on her own behalf.[4]

While a first issue for victims is validation of their experiences and feelings, a second issue is *confidentiality*. Victims have had to cover bruises, scars, tears, cuts, or public outbursts. In order to survive and keep the family together, they have had to give the appearance of a happy, normal, and loving family. This is an expectation and burden that the abuser has placed upon the victim. The victim feels that it is her responsibility to keep the violence quiet and hidden from the public. Many times they have paid the price for others hearing or seeing the abuser attack them. They also carry a sense of shame for living in this relationship. When a victim shares her suffering, she

2. Nason-Clark, *The Battered Wife*, 41. Adams indicates that victims want someone to listen to them and acknowledge their suffering (Adams, *Woman-Battering*, 38).

3. "Chronic mistreatment gets people to doubt themselves. Children of abusive parents know that something is wrong, but they suspect the badness is inside of them. Employees of an abusive boss spend much of their time feeling that they are doing a lousy job, that they should be smarter and work harder. Boys who get bullied feel that they should be stronger or less afraid to fight" (Bancroft, *Why Does He Do That?* 49).

4. Weitzman, *"Not to People Like Us,"* 35.

is risking her own safety as well as her own emotional security. Victims may share their deepest pain with someone and never return for help. The fear of public humiliation and shame keeps them from seeking help. The abuser has convinced them that public exposure is bad for the victim, when in reality it is the reverse.

Third, victims want *peace and safety*: "I just want him to stop hitting me" is a phrase I hear women say to judges as they submit a restraining order. Children, when taken out of the home, just want the abuse to end. No victim asks to be mistreated. They resist outsiders threatening or punishing the abuser. They want to protect the abuser, but they also want to be protected in their own right. Countless women never tell their fathers or brothers when their husbands or boyfriends abuse them. "If my father would have known I was being abused, he would have killed him!" As a father myself, I can understand the passion of their fathers. Why not tell dads about the abuse? Because they love their partners, and they do not want to be alone. They also expect condemnation from friends and family who ask, "How could you have married such an abuser?" The victim hopes that the abuse will stop, and that peace will be restored to the family. They love this person and are committed to him. She may see herself as the problem and just want peace.

Finally victims *want to be loved*. They truly hope for the best and believe that the partner can change. Many victims have had a history of intimate relationships with men who have been abusive, but this does not mean that they seek abuse. One member in the church where I preached said, "I don't know why they just don't get out. They must enjoy being treated this way." This was an insensitive comment, made out of ignorance. Abusers are manipulators, and they have a powerful way of making victims feel that they are being loved. Victims are like all of us—they want to be loved and respected. They, like anyone else, deserve this. Their hesitance to leave an abusive relationship may come from a fear of being rejected and unloved.

Fear, finances, and fantasy of change are three additional reasons why women do not leave their abusers.[5] While women may fear their husbands, they also believe that their husbands will change, or that they can change their husbands. What happens when they leave their abuser? They have to raise their child, find a job, and live in transition. They are at greater risk of being attacked or killed by their partner. They feel at times as if they made a mistake to have become involved in an abusive relationship to begin with. Then they come to church and see families that seem happy. They hear sermons on how people divorce too easily, or they hear that adultery is the only scriptural

5. Kroeger and Nason-Clark, *No Place for Abuse*, 34–35.

ground for divorce. They hear how wives must submit to their husbands and through patience and submission can turn them around. These women feel alone and out of place. They feel guilty about and responsible for the direction of their marriages. Instead of feeling that they have made a wise choice to leave a partner, they feel ashamed, and feel that they are failures. They hear the abuser's voice from the pulpit saying, "You can't leave me, because no one will accept you." Even though the abusive relationship is dangerous, they feel a sense of love, support, and acceptance in that relationship.

Were you ever bullied by another person when you were younger?

- How did you react?
- While others said it's not that bad, was it real in your mind?
- Did you worry every time you saw the bully?
- When he/she stared at you, did you feel overwhelmed with fear?
- When he made a punching motion with his hand, or when she acted like she was going to slap you, did you react defensively?
- How many teachers did you tell?
- Do you remember the warning "If you tell anyone I will get you after school"?
- If the teacher asked if you were okay, in front of the bully, what did you say?
- Above all, how did it feel when the bully came to you and acted as if everything was good?
- How did it feel when she put her arm around you and acted like she was your friend?

Remember that sigh of relief mixed with uneasiness? "Good," you thought, "today is a day I won't get pummeled!"

> Most of us start a relationship thinking we have certain limits in terms of what we will or won't tolerate from other people. But as the relationship progresses, we tend to move our boundaries back, giving in more and more until we end up tolerating more and more and even doing things we were determined not to do. Not only do we begin tolerating unacceptable and abusive behavior, we begin to convince ourselves that these behaviors are normal or acceptable.[6]

6. Engel, *The Emotionally Abused Woman*, 159.

Abuse victims live on that playground every day, and they usually won't tell a soul, because they know what will happen when no teachers are around. Yet whenever a teacher intervenes and protects them, while they may resist, deep down the victims appreciate the help.

One of my favorite Dr. Seuss stories is *Horton Hears a Who*. In the story Horton, an elephant with big ears, hears a cry from a Who person in a tiny city that exists on a small flower. Throughout the story Horton listens and speaks to these unknown tiny people. When the community where Horton lives tries to destroy the flower, not knowing the Who people, Horton tries to convince them that these people exist. The community does not believe Horton and continues the plan to destroy the flower. Finally, Horton convinces the Who people to make so much noise that the friends of Horton hear them. The city is saved because someone with *big ears* hears the cries of the little people and convinces others that they exist.

God has big ears and hears the cries of the oppressed and abused (Ps 95:1–9; Jonah 4:9–11). While faith communities have at times been oblivious to the voice of the little people, God continues to challenge Christians to hear their cries. When the faith community supports women who are being abused, it needs to *validate* the victims by listening to their story and showing empathy.

> A woman cannot escape an abusive marriage unless she first realizes that she is being battered and puts a name to her situation. Often this insight comes through others . . . Most women report that it was input from external sources—friends, relatives, therapists, lawyers, even strangers—that ultimately helped them recognize they were in an abusive marriage and gave them the courage and permission to get out.
>
> When others witness or comment on abusive behaviors, the little voice that the upscale abused wife once heard inside her and ignored or muffled becomes amplified. Slowly she starts to recognize that she must stop enduring the abuse.[7]

The community also needs to appreciate the great risk that these victims have taken when they share their story. It is the victim's right to expect *confidentiality* until they decide to share their story with others. The faith community should also be concerned about providing *peace and safety* to the women who seek help. Finally, the spiritual community has a great opportunity to show *love* and *acceptance* to those who have been abused. It is the responsibility of the faith community to listen, protect, love, and provide safety to

7. Weitzman, *"Not to People Like Us,"* 112–15.

victims. We must empower them to be strong rather than humiliate them back into submission, self-blame, and fear.

Abusers

Since we have defined domestic violence as power and control rather than anger, it is important to discuss the major issues that abusers face. The power and control issues are such that even an outsider can get caught in the web of manipulation, coercion, and control. Abusers are not monsters. They are human beings whose views of life are dysfunctional and need reform.[8]

First, abusive partners usually feel that *they are the victims*. The world of the abuser is one that revolves around him. Abusers tend to be narcissistic and have the feeling that they are being victimized in the domestic-violence justice system. Perceiving themselves as victims, they feel that their actions are always in response to others. If other people would behave, they often reason, they would not lose their temper or become violent. Abusers spend much of their lives reacting to the actions of others rather than practicing self-control.

Second, abusers *attempt to control* others because they are concerned about self-image. This may stem from low self-esteem or deep insecurities. They may practice control in different ways, but they do attempt to control others. While the abusive man may seem like the perfect gentleman in public, he is controlling how others view him. No one would know that he goes home and beats his wife or verbally humiliates her. Her family may see him as a nice guy. If he ever explodes in public, he will quickly try to smooth over his actions to others, while later taking it out on his partner behind closed doors. *Men who are violent outside the home usually are violent within the home, yet men who are violent within the home usually are not violent outside the family.* When pressure is on the family (the wife leaves, the children tell someone about the abuse, or the husband feels others know about the problem), the abuser will become very concerned to persuade others that it is not his fault. He may suggest that he was overstressed or sleep deprived, or that it was just this once. He may also tell others that it was her fault by saying, "She attacked me, and I was defending myself." Excuses and perceptions are important to the abuser because he is concerned about self-image.

8. Bancroft, *Why Does He Do That?* 36.

"I was told by my sister-in-law to call you," the voice said on the telephone. I had never met him but had seen his picture. It was the family picture I glanced at as we persuaded his wife to get the two children and leave for her parents' home. Her sister was a member of our congregation, and we had worked up this escape plan for a few weeks. We helped her out that day, and he was calling me that night.

"What do you want to talk about?" I said.

"Well, I'm really hurtin' here. My wife left and won't talk to me. She took the kids away from me. She says I have been verbally abusive to her and had some anger problems. She says I neglect them because I won't work and when I'm home I won't help her out around the house."

"Anything else?" I asked.

"Yes, I guess I have hit her sometimes but I was drunk," he finally said.

"Why are you calling me?" I asked.

"My sister-in-law told me maybe you can help. Says you work with this stuff."

"Yes, I do," I said. "To be honest with you, I was there to get your wife out."

There was silence on the phone, then he said, "Thank you for doing that—I know you care about me and my family. I only want the best for them."

"Thank you," I said. "I think we need to talk, and I would like you to come to my office tomorrow."

"I want to. By the way Brother Ron [I didn't know he was religious] from my study of the Bible she can't leave me unless I have an affair on her. From what my mom told me, Jesus said she is not to divorce me. Do you think we should study that tomorrow? Maybe she can come in and we can look at that together?"

"Oh," I said. "Actually, I think she can leave you for other reasons. We'll study some of those passages if you would like."

Again silence on the phone.

I then interrupted the silence. "Todd, I know that you care about your wife but understand that God does not tolerate certain behaviors. Drugs, drunkenness, pornography, verbal humiliation, physical violence, and child neglect are all behaviors that God does not want your wife and children to experience in their home. I think that God wants them to have something better. Don't you agree?"

Again silence on the phone.

"I guess you're right. Maybe we need to talk," he said.

"How about tomorrow morning? In fact why don't we have prayer right now?" I said.

Abusers are not monsters. They are trying to persuade people that they are good and do not need to change. Working with them requires wisdom, compassion, and discernment.

Abusers feel victimized, and they attempt to control others. But abusers also use manipulation to confuse those suffering abuse. While potential victims experience fear around an abuser, verbal and psychological abuse can confuse not only victims but also those working to reform abusers. Abusers may use intimidation and manipulation in situations where these strategies work for them. They may also use self-pity and try to evoke sympathy from those around them: "I guess you really don't care about me," or "I guess you think you're perfect enough to judge me" are common statements abusers make. Sometimes they blame: "Haven't you ever made a mistake?" Other times they can talk circles around another person in an attempt to coerce and convince the person that the evidence against them is slight and one-sided. I call this the headache syndrome, because it gives me a headache, while other intervention specialists call it "crazy making" behavior. Victims are confused by the "Jekyll and Hyde" personality and find themselves unsure of their own feelings and of their perception of a situation.

> When an abuser denies an incident immediately after it happens, he can set his partner's head spinning. Picture a woman who arises in the morning with her stomach still tied in a knot from an ugly blowout the night before. Her partner makes a face at her in the kitchen and says, "Why are you so grumpy today?" . . . The more serious the incidents he denies, the more her grip on reality can start to slip. And if outsiders start to notice her instability, the abuser can use their observations to persuade them that her revelations of abuse by him are fantasies.[9]

Third, the abuser is *dominated by fear*. The abuse of power is motivated by fear and a desire to control the lives of others.[10] This may seem odd to the observer, because these men appear to be in control, but they are narcissistic. They are concerned about their public image and are trying to cover up their deep-seated fears of rejection and low self-esteem. They fear being alone or abandoned. While they are trying to gain control, they are actually losing it. They are the heroes of their own stories because they need to be honored and praised by those closest to them. They seek validation because they know that their behavior is unacceptable. I believe that they want to change, but change brings discomfort and fear.

9. Bancroft, *Why Does He Do That?* 72.
10. Poling, *The Abuse of Power*, 27.

Finally, abusers are *not in touch with their true feelings*. Many males have been taught as children that the only emotion they can show is anger. They are in denial concerning their abusive behavior and justify or minimize this sin. As with many young men, peacefulness, negotiation, and a willingness to ignore humiliation are seen as weaknesses rather than strengths. Unfortunately, some societies, including that of the United States, communicate to young men that certain behaviors are associated with being a man. This message is also present in media and culture. Behaviors are deemed male or female.[11] I also find that this dichotomy of emotions is prevalent in some of the Christian marriage literature. While men and women have some physiological differences, I feel that we have much in common.

> A second myth—especially when we read popular articles or books about gender difference—lumps all men into one category and all women into the opposite category. It turns out that there is as much diversity *within* a group of women or *within* a group of men as there is *between* men and women. This has been shown to be true in studies of math skills, verbal skills, aggression, and spatial abilities. The *between-group* difference is smaller than the *within-group* difference.[12]

In some of the popular books about males and females, men are considered the hunters and gatherers and women the homemakers.[13]

This is clear even in popular Christian literature. For example, the book *Wild At Heart: Discovering the Passionate Soul of a Man* by John Eldredge laments the fact that men have become peaceful and compassionate:

> Society at large can't make up its mind about men. Having spent the last thirty years redefining masculinity into something more sensitive, safe, manageable and, well, feminine, it now berates men for not being men. Boys will be boys, they sigh. As though if a man were to truly grow up he would forsake wilderness and wanderlust and settle down, be at home forever in Aunt Polly's parlor. "Where are all the real men?" is regular fare for talk shows and new books. You asked them to be women, I want to say. The result is a gender confusion never experienced at such a wide level in the history of the world. How can a man know he is one when his highest aim is minding his manners?[14]

11. Kivel, *Men's Work*, 21, 44.

12. Mathews, *Preaching that Speaks to Women*, 24.

13. Probably the most common book is Gray, *Men Are from Mars, Women Are from Venus*.

14. Eldredge, *Wild At Heart*, 6–7.

Eldredge suggests that it is in the nature of men to be like God, but his view of God seems to be cultural. Men are designed to be violent, restless, and aggressive. In his mind, men are to be warriors, like God.

> Capes and swords, camouflage, bandannas and six-shooters—these are the uniforms of boyhood. Little boys yearn to know they are powerful, they are dangerous, they are someone to be reckoned with . . . If we believe that man is made in the image of God, then we would do well to remember that "the LORD is a warrior, the LORD is his name" (Exod 15:3).[15]

Alas, the author continues to suggest that our problem today is that we as men have become *feminized* or *emasculated*. We are restless because deep down we want to be daring, aggressive, tough, and heroic. We should be warriors, not just good boys. These are the characteristics that Eldredge defines as truly masculine.

> To most men, God is either distant or he is weak—the very thing they'd report of their earthly fathers. Be honest now—what is your image of Jesus as a man? "Isn't he sort of meek and mild?" a friend remarked. "I mean the pictures I have of him show a gentle guy with children all around. Kind of like Mother Teresa." Yes, those are the pictures I've seen myself in many churches. In fact, those are the only pictures I've seen of Jesus. As I've said before, they leave me with the impression that he was the world's nicest guy. Mister Rogers with a beard. Telling me to be like him feels like telling me to go limp and passive. Be nice. Be swell. Be like Mother Teresa. I'd much rather be told to be like William Wallace.[16]

Eldredge seems to suggest that we have the feminists to blame for this problem. Instead of teaching us to model the truly great virtues of love, compassion, and mercy, Eldredge suggests that feminists have taken away our manhood by making us become "good boys." Yet most of the men I work with resent their fathers for being the stereotypical male. In the movie *The Big Fish*, the son was angry at his father for being too involved in the adventure and telling the big story and not concerned enough about listening to his own son. Most men I know respect the dad who was home, holding the children, and being an example of a good husband.

As I read through Eldredge's book, I couldn't help but wonder if the author received his images of manhood from real life or from the movies. His quota-

15. Ibid., 10.
16. Ibid., 22.

tion of *Braveheart* suggests to me that his image of William Wallace was more from Mel Gibson than it was from history. His distaste for Mother Teresa and Mr. Rogers slaps women and compassionate men in the face.

It is this very mindset that we are fighting in domestic-violence intervention ministry. This mindset suggests that certain behaviors are feminine or masculine. This mindset causes men to be afraid of showing qualities that others, such as Eldredge, consider feminine. One of the victims' advocates on our abuse council, who is also a former victim, asked me if I had read *Wild at Heart*. When I expressed my opinion, she agreed and said she was aggravated when she read it and would not want her son to get a copy. This has also been the sentiment of many batter-intervention advocates. Eldredge suggested in his book that women want a hero, yet my wife responded, "Girls want a hero; women want a man who is a good husband and father." Yet this is an example of how cultural and worldly thinking have crept into the church. This thinking warps the view of God and requires Jesus to be Rambo.

Labeling feelings and behavior as male or female can keep men from becoming like God. When men are asked what feelings are associated with masculinity, a box is created with those emotions and feelings (Figure 4). A real man, according to many young men, is tough, strong, sexy, independent, and the like.

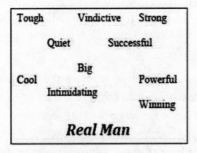

Figure 4: **Definition of a Real Man?** Used by permission of Paul Kivel (http://www.paulkivel.com/) and the Oakland Men's Project © 1983.

The emotions outside the box, which are opposite those inside the box, are considered feminine (Figure 5). Thus, those who are not real men are weak, a failure, submissive, dependant, and loving.

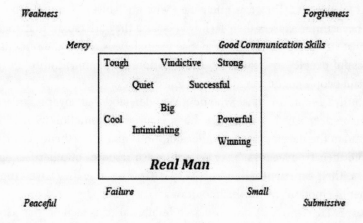

Figure 5: Behaviors Outside the Box. Used by permission of Paul Kivel (http://www.paulkivel
.com/) and the Oakland Men's Project © 1983.

Our masculine culture has a way of reinforcing these "masculine emotions" by using degrading terms to force men to stay inside the box (Figure
6). Those behaviors opposite "real man's" behavior are labeled female or
homosexual.

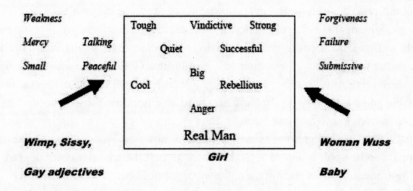

Figure 6: Staying Inside the Box. Used by permission of Paul Kivel (http://www.paulkivel.com/)
and the Oakland Men's Project © 1983.

If a young man steps outside the box, he is humiliated and labeled a
woman, a sissy, gay, or the like. Because of this, many men grow up frustrated
because they cannot be themselves and practice the variety of emotions that
reflects the image and glory of God. They learn to fear those who are the "opposite" of them. This is possibly the source for misogyny and homophobia.
Men fear women because they practice the very emotions that men have been

taught to suppress. They fear other men who are labeled "feminine" by others. They cannot express their feelings because they are taught that anger is the most culturally acceptable response to anxiety. Anger is the response of "successful people" or "real men." Intimidation and humiliation result from powerful people conquering the weak in a display of anger.

Abusive people are those who do not understand that anger is a reaction to their anxiety. Anger seems to be the most prevalent emotion in their lives. This stunts the development of other emotions and gives them permission to avoid their true feelings. They do not have a resource of other feelings to process. Their experiences of life are very narrow because they have a limited number of emotions from which to draw.

This is far removed from God. While biblical texts suggest that God is passionate and at times gets angry (Exod 32:11; Num 11:1; John 2:12–19), God grieves, relents, and is vulnerable (Gen 6:6; Exod 32:14; John 11:34). God continues to reach out to those who would bring grief because of their disobedience, and remains faithful. In a dialogue with Moses, Yahweh reveals a nature that is compassionate, gracious, slow to anger, abounding in love and faithfulness, maintaining love to thousands, and forgiving of wickedness, rebellion, and sin (Exod 34:6–7). Yet Yahweh does punish the guilty. God is not a God of anger but of compassion, love, and *mercy*. God may be passionate about people but this passion is shown in a desire for relationship.

Many of these characteristics of God came to men (Exod 34:6–7; Jonah 4:2). That God is conceived of as male in our culture is not discrimination against women but a revelation to men about a God whose nature is considered feminine in other cultures. In a world that separated male and female gods, to supply the "male" and "female" emotions, Yahweh needed no separation. Yahweh is one because Yahweh can practice both discipline and patience. God understood as male brought a message to men, who needed to practice the noble qualities of God's nature in their lives. God was not degrading women but was teaching men how they should behave. God as Father is simply God as a model for fathers. Jesus as a son is a model for the church of God. Christ as the bridegroom of the church is a model for husbands. In a world of male violence, God reveals to men that spirituality is about patience, love, compassion, mercy, and faith. When men think of God as masculine, they learn that male nature is grounded in God rather than in culture.

When the faith community attempts to work with abusers, these issues need to be remembered. Abusers feel victimized, attempt to control others, are struggling with fear, and have trouble communicating their true feelings. They are not the enemy. They are not to be demonized, but loved. They are human beings who have been misguided and stunted from growing in the image of God.

> What lies at the core of reconciliation is nothing less than the enchanting and overwhelming notion that even when a human has become so distorted and disfigured by egoism, rage, despair, and fear, that person will be embraced by the Christian community. The Christian community has within its treasure trove of symbols a call for reconciliation. We are called as Christians not to demonize those who act in evil ways but rather to call them to accountability and to love them. This required that we ferret out the true insights in this message of hope.[17]

The media and society have done a good job of bringing abuse awareness into the communities. Yet in the popular imagination there tends to be a sense of anger and vindictiveness toward abusers. A popular musical group has written a song about a woman who kills her husband. The song mentions that "Earl had to die." When we meet violence with anger and rage, we also become abusers. When we fail to understand the abuser's fears and emotional immaturity, we intimidate him and attempt to enforce compliance.

One of the greatest dangers facing those who work with abusers is the danger of being caught in the abuser's web of confusion. We should be careful that we do not enable him or become manipulated by him. On the other hand, we need to be careful that we are not dominated by the same fear that he experiences. Too often media and popular culture have chosen to meet abusers with anger and vengeance. The vigilantes become the heroes and judges of our society. This reflects our own sense of helplessness and fear. Ignorance and insecurity cannot address power and control issues. Abusers, like victims, need love, peace, acceptance, and safety. The faith community must be innocent as doves and wise as serpents (Matt 10:16). The church must support victims by calling abusers to accountability.

> Abusive men choose when and how to be abusive. They could choose not to rape their wives anally, not to throw them down the stairs, not to threaten them verbally or emotionally. But abusive men profit from their behavior. Their partners quit jobs or take jobs, get pregnant or have abortions, cut themselves off from their friends, keep the kids quiet at times or send them away. Men who batter not only believe they have the right to use violence, but receive rewards for behaving in this manner, namely, obedience and loyalty. In addition, battering guarantees that the man wins disputes that the status quo in the relationship is maintained, and that the woman will not leave him.[18]

17. Livingston, *Healing Violent Men*, 65.
18. Adams, *Woman-Battering*, 20.

Children in Abusive Homes

Power and control issues also affect children who live in abusive homes. The purpose of this book is not to address child abuse but to address the effects of intimate partner violence on children. When children experience or observe verbal abuse and violence, their emotional and physical development is greatly affected. Studies have shown that children in violent homes suffer from a form of posttraumatic stress disorder (PTSD).[19] PTSD affects children continually and can cause *hypervigilance*. Children may experience nightmares or have recurring flashbacks of violent or traumatic events that they have observed or experienced. PTSD can also cause the children to behave in one of two ways.

First, children may react to trauma with *hyperarousal*. Hyperarousal is a state in which children experience high levels of anxiety. This will affect them physiologically in ways such as increased heart rate, clenched fists, standing up or pacing, intense fear, or anger. Mentally they will begin to cross the threshold of their brain activity, which causes their blood flow to increase to the outer extremities of their body. This "fight or flight" response decreases the blood flow to the rational/logical portion of the brain.[20] These children can be aroused easily and react irrationally to a perceived threat. If anger is a dominant emotion for young children, it will be used frequently. When under trauma, they become edgy and anxious. This would explain some forms of attention deficit disorder (ADD) and sleep difficulties that children who witness abuse often exhibit. I have heard that small children have attacked their mother's abuser without any understanding of disproportionate strength or size and without concern about being harmed.

Another reaction from children is *disassociation*. This is the opposite of hyperarousal, in that the child retreats from the real world and experiences isolation and a denial of their emotions. They put away their feelings and go into hiding. This is more prevalent in younger children and adolescent females. They come to the realization that they are helpless to change the situation, so they move away from it.

> Consequently, traumatic experiences can result in people cutting themselves off emotionally and psychically from others and themselves. . . .

19. Martin, *Critical Problems in Children and Youth*, 143–44. See also the Boston Medical Center website which suggests that 80–85 percent of children who witnessed violence in the home suffer from mild PTSD.

20. "When animals are threatened or perceive danger, they do respond in ways that we liken to anger: hair (if the animal has hair) stands on end, pupils dilate, muscles tense, fins flap, warning growls or chirps or rattles sound, and the organism readies itself to fight or flee" (Tavris, *Anger*, 34).

In this way, human-induced trauma naturally propels persons into a state of being radically disconnected, and also keeps them stuck in a state of social isolation from others and psychological isolation from themselves. Persons who have a history of being abused, neglected, and isolated in these ways are often prone to perpetrate similar abuse and neglect on others.[21]

Children in abusive families also *experience learning and cognitive disorders* by being exposed to abusers and spousal abuse. Lundy Bancroft lists the following psychological symptoms of children exposed to domestic violence:[22]

- Attention deficits
- Hyperactivity that interferes with learning and attention
- Learning delays
- Delays in language acquisition
- Poor academic performance
- Missing school often through sickness or truancy
- Falling asleep in school
- Sibling rivalry or hierarchy

Bancroft indicates that these traits are not just due to witnessing domestic violence. He indicates that exposure to an abuser may cause children to also be easily manipulated, to suffer traumatic bonding, and to become involved in undermining their mother.

Children are emotionally affected by living in abuse. While much work has been done to protect the women in abusive situations and provide for their safety, children many times are exposed to the abuser even after he is taken out of the house. Unsupervised visitation makes it possible for the abuser to continue to undermine the woman and manipulate her into taking him back or letting him take the children.

Parental conflict has a destructive impact on the emotional well-being of children. Parents may think that children are not aware of the abuse, but they do hear and sense the conflict that exists in the home. "Children learn to recognize ominous tones of voice and intimidating body language. They feel sharp pains when they see their mother humiliated or degraded. They are filled with an urgent desire to rescue her, but at the same time can feel paralyzed

---

21. Means, *Trauma & Evil*, 24.

22. Bancroft, *When Dad Hurts Mom*, 76, 145–46.

by fear, so they are left feeling guilty standing by and not intervening. Their innocence can slip away in the process."[23]

The words from the song "Wonderful," by a popular Portland, Oregon, band Everclear, summarize the stress that children of abuse face in the home. Children react to trauma and stress in different ways. They may seem normal on the outside, but they internalize much of what they are witnessing.[24] Educators understand that hyperarousal and disassociation are prevalent in children from abusive and dysfunctional homes.

Children of abuse have not developed the skills to process their experiences, as most healing adults have done. As the children grow, they use only the skills that they have developed. Hyperarousal becomes hypervigilance. Fear, intimidation, and anger do not affect or control hypervigilant children. Abusive parents can control smaller children through threats and violence, but adolescents who have learned to disassociate ignore these consequences.

> Various life experiences can disrupt one's developing concept of self, world, others, and God. They do this by disrupting the interpersonal environments in which the basic structures influencing one's attitudes and orientation to self and the world are formed. Experiences of human-induced trauma and neglect massively distort these interpersonal relationships, damage developing mental structures, and subsequently have a continuing deleterious impact on a person's development and interactions with others.
>
> The effect of such abuse and neglect upon children is especially devastating. This is in part because a child's self-structure and defenses are weak and in the early stages of formation. Children also lack fully developed cognitive capacities, so they are even less able to understand what is happening to them than are adults in similar circumstances. Children are also more severely damaged by the tremendous power differential existing between themselves and significant adults.[25]

One should never use intimidation, fear, humiliation, shame, or threats with children. We must practice compassion and mercy, and must empower children to discuss their feelings and increase their threshold of patience. Children exposed to abuse are traumatized and resist or withdraw from authority. Children must know that the church can be a place to ask any questions and share experiences with confidentiality, no matter how horrible they are. They must also know that they will be believed and heard without being judged.

23. Ibid, 13.
24. Thompson, "An Interview with James Garbarino," 8–9.
25. Means, *Trauma & Evil*, 24.

Family and Friends

While many of my experiences are with victims, often family and friends seek help for those who are in violent relationships. Family and friends also face issues that cause them to be concerned about their loved ones. Many experience the same emotions that victims do. *Shock and disbelief* usually are first on the list of issues. I find that most have attempted to accept the abuser into their family and have been manipulated into thinking that "he has a few rough edges but nothing serious." Others have accepted the victim into their family and are shocked that someone would ever mistreat someone they love. I think that much of this shock and disbelief happens because we demonize abusers rather than understand that they are products of a dysfunctional system.

Shame is another issue that family or friends may experience: "How could I have been so blind?" is a common response. In retrospect, family members and friends believe that they ignored red flags and begin to feel responsible. Others had seen it coming and feel that there was more that they should have done. Some are embarrassed that their children are having marital problems or are caught up in family violence. Members of the dysfunctional family may see the dysfunction as a threat to their honor, as something to be quieted: "We need to take care of our own, and it is our responsibility to set him/her straight." This type of thinking further contributes to the problem, as discussed in the next chapter.

Finally *anger* is an issue that family and friends may face. In Genesis 34, Shechem rapes Dinah, the daughter of Jacob. Shechem's father, Hamor, comes to negotiate a bride price or settlement with Jacob. Shechem takes over the negotiations and wants to bargain for Dinah. Because Jacob is silent during the negotiations, Dinah's brothers decide to manipulate and take vengeance on Shechem and his village. The brothers suggest that the Shechemites have every male circumcised before agreeing to a marriage between Dinah and Shechem. On the third day after the circumcisions, when all the Shechemites are sore from the surgery, the sons of Jacob slaughter all the men in an act of vigilantism. The brothers' anger may have been justified in their minds, but Dinah was never consulted and the Scriptures give no indication whether or not she was helped or validated.[26] Vigilantism is a response by people who feel powerless over the fact that justice has not been achieved.

Those counseling families need to remind them that the abuse is not about the family; it is about helping those directly affected by the violence. Victims

---

26. For a deeper discussion of the text as well as other opinions of the rape-of-Dinah story, see Clark, "The Silence in Dinah's Cry," 81–98.

need understanding, patience, peace, and safety, not vengeance. Abusers need accountability, not anger. Children need a safe place to process what is happening. While it is difficult to stay calm, difficult not to react angrily, and difficult to listen, these are what family and friends need to practice. Domestic violence is not about them; it is about the victim, the children, and the abuser. The faith community must see the deeper issues in domestic violence. The faith community is not God, but a representation of God. God judges; the community empowers the family to heal. Victims must be supported, protected, and validated. Abusers must be confronted and called to see the needs of others rather than their own needs. Children need a place to unwind and feel safe. Family and friends need to learn how to help the family heal as a relational and emotional system.

The faith community can become the family needed for healing. The abuser and victim should each have a separate faith community for healing and spiritual growth. Power and control issues are so complex that a couple caught in domestic violence will have a difficult time healing in the same congregation. The couple never should be counseled together until the victim is empowered enough to confront the abuser. Each needs to experience the acceptance and care of a faith community so that each can focus on healing. Faith communities can work together to help abusers and victims heal, but victims must have their own place of support, protection, and safety.

If a victim is separated from her abuser, she must be able to attend church without fear of manipulation or pressure to reunite. Victims must have validation from their church in order to grow closer to God and find healing. Abusers must also have accountability and support from their church in order to develop and heal spiritually. They must be able to attend church without fear of rejection or the temptation to manipulate their partner back into a relationship. They must also be accountable not to seek another victim.[27] Since much of their self-esteem is related to an intimate relationship, they need to know that relationships with other nonabusive men are important to their healing and repentance. They have the right to belong to a community that reminds them they are not in control, that challenges them to repent of sin, and that encourages them to validate other victims. Churches can work with one another to see the progress of individuals. This will take patience and understanding, but it can be done to the glory of God, who calls all people to seek truth and healthy relationships.

27. Bancroft, *Why Does He Do That?* 121.

CHAPTER 3

How Does Domestic Violence
Affect Families?

THE PREVIOUS CHAPTER addressed some of the issues that domestic-violence victims face. This chapter will introduce some of the effects that domestic violence can have on families and family members. Historically little has been done to protect women in abusive relationships.[1] The burden has been placed on the victim to report the incident, press charges, find help, and survive on her own or with her family.

> Compassion for abused women is building across the continent, but we are still a society with deep habits of blaming victims. When people suffer misfortune, we jump to analyzing what they should have done differently: She should have fought back, she shouldn't have fought back; she was in an area where it wasn't wise to be walking; she didn't plan ahead; she didn't try hard enough or think fast enough.[2]

At times the church has failed to support victims in domestic violence.

> Ultimately the blame is widespread, for Christian believers worldwide tend to ignore, minimize and deny the abuse that is rampant in families of faith. Churches provide few resources for victims of abuse. Moreover, believers are discouraged from using available community services such as shelters, counseling, abusers' groups, restraining orders and legal aid. Without such help, the abuse frequently grows more severe. The potential of emotional and spiritual healing is sacrificed to silence. Silence of the sacred. *Sacred silence.*[3]

With increased awareness of domestic violence, with availability of resources, with women's rights in divorce and birth control, and with the ability of the police (rather than the victim) to press charges, it seems that women

---

1. Engel, "Historical Theology and Violence against Women," 242–61; Johnson and Bondurant, "Revisiting the 1982 Church Response Survey," 422–27.

2. Bancroft, *When Dad Hurts Mom*, 313.

3. Kroeger and Nason-Clark, *No Place for Abuse*, 7–8.

have more options available to them concerning abusive and dysfunctional relationships. There has also been an increase in support from abuse agencies, counselors, and legal services; government funding to protect victims and hold abusers accountable; and prevention programs. The increase in resources for women may also be responsible for the decrease in the number of men murdered by their intimate partners.[4] The presence of abuse in gay and lesbian relationships and increased reports concerning male victims suggest that power and control are not limited to one gender. Intimate-partner violence also affects those close to the couple. Research provides much more information on how the family is affected by this trauma and violence. Families are a system which adapts to trauma, dysfunction, and outside pressure.

Family Systems Theory

The family is a system or group that seeks equilibrium. Family members form an emotional unit.[5] Within the emotional unit each member places an emphasis on shared responsibility, repeated patterns, and mutual support physically and emotionally.[6] Members of the family live together and try to maintain balance in the system. A healthy family cultivates love, encouragement, and emotional support, and addresses dysfunction as a team.

Dysfunctional Families and Family Systems Theory

Some families cope with dysfunction by using resources within the system. If a parent or child begins to hurt a member inside the system, the family may adapt through isolation, reframing, keeping secrets, using language barriers, or expelling those who interact with the environment or an outsider. The family unit develops its own system of ethics, wholeness, and health in order to protect its honor. The emotional unit revolves around the leader, who may be the source of the problem, and the group often sees reality through that individual's perspective. Dysfunctional families do not practice shared power, and they have an imbalance of power and emotion when the leader is abusive.

---

4. While the number of women murdered by their intimate partners stabilized from 1976 to 1993, the number of men murdered by their intimate partners decreased 60 percent from 1976 to 1993 and 23 percent from 1993 to 1997. In the past, many women found that killing their abusive partner was the only way of escape. The decrease in the number of male homicides suggests that many abused women had other options than killing their abuser. See Rennison and Welchans, *Intimate Partner Violence*, 3.

5. Kerr and Bowen, *Family Evaluation*, 7.

6. Becvar and Becvar, *Family Therapy*, 9.

In abusive families, members adapt in order to survive. In this system, one parent usually has attempted to exercise control and power over all family members. In order to protect the children, the other spouse may try to hide the abuse from them. The protective spouse may also "overfunction" to shield others in the family. The term *enabler* has traditionally been used for this role, but I have found that *enabler* has a negative slant. Rather than *enable*, I prefer to use words such as *adapt* or *overfunction*. These women have a strong will to survive, and they do whatever it takes to establish peace and to avoid further abuse. They put themselves at great risk by adapting and surviving within a dysfunctional emotional system. The abuser, who "underfunctions," is the one who determines the health of the family. He is attempting to control the family, and the members are expected to follow his wishes. I have met women who work a full-time job, take care of children, and keep the house clean while their abusive husband fails to find or keep a job, to clean the house, or to share in the parenting. She doesn't know what he does all day at home and wonders why he constantly sleeps, spends money, and creates debt for the family. Yet he has convinced his wife that it is everyone else's fault that he can't work, and that it is her responsibility to keep the family together by her work and service to him. On top of this, he demands sex when he desires it. Women under this level of stress still communicate to me that God expects them to serve and support their husbands no matter how they feel about the relationship. A woman in this situation overfunctions not because she desires to do so, but because her husband (and many times her church) has convinced her that she is responsible for the stability of the marriage.

The abuser also determines spoken and unspoken rules of conduct. Family members learn by trial and error what is acceptable and what is unacceptable. Those outside the family have no bearing on what is normal. While outsiders may see who underfunctions and manipulates, they are considered to have a warped view of family. The one in power makes decisions concerning what is normal. Those behaviors that serve and show respect to the head of the family are honorable. Those that do not are punishable through violence, verbal abuse, or threats of expulsion from the family.

One of the greatest fears that I hear from victims involves being cut off and disengaged from their families. I have seen adult survivors of molestation point the finger at their abuser only to be criticized and isolated from siblings and the other parent even if they also have been victimized. I have seen wives take a stand against their husbands for abuse only to later be pressured by in-laws to take him back. I have known of preachers who *excommunicate or disfellowship* abused wives for filing restraining orders against their husbands, who are "fellow brothers." Isolation, disengagement, and expulsion are used to shame and humiliate victims who oppose the honor of the abusive, dysfunctional family. The one in control dominates the emotional unit and manipulates those outside the family to support and honor his wishes. Only those outsiders considered worthy by the underfunctioning individual (which means that they agree with him) can enter the unit.

Outsiders are usually viewed as a threat to the family caught in abuse. Outsiders bring the threat of exposure, and family members are groomed to keep the honor of the family. When a member marries, the new relationship brings great danger to the abuser and to the dysfunctional system. According to the abuser, honor must be maintained. Many times the abuser will manipulate the outsider and gain their respect and favor.

> They had been attending church for almost a year. Karen and her second husband, Scott, had been friends with us for a long time and we knew their children well. They had been married eight years. While we were visiting in their home one evening, Karen shared with us why she did not believe in God. Her stepfather had molested her until she turned twelve. She had asked God for help, but it never came. It broke our hearts to hear the words she spoke and to see Scott's frustration. Scott had been told this after they had been married for three years. He couldn't say anything to the stepfather. They lived next door to him, Karen worked for him, and they spent a lot of family time together. Yet Scott, the outsider, was given a "gag" order. Karen felt sorry for her stepfather and believed he had changed, or at least she hoped he had, because their children spent the night at "grandma's and grandpa's" often. Day after day Scott faced the man who caused his wife such pain, and through clenched teeth he had to be cordial and *act as if he did not know or suspect anything.* He had to, because the man had given them their home!

This is an example of the code of silence in abusive families. It is a method of control and manipulation in order to honor and serve the abuser. It keeps the family and in-laws "in line." This seems foreign to an outsider but is a normal way of life to those groomed and manipulated to keep the peace.

The times my wife and I visited with Karen's stepfather were difficult. We went to our kids' sporting events together and spent time sitting with their family. We knew what he had done, yet he was very charming, attentive, and encouraging. They had the appearance of one big happy family. From the outside, the family members were lucky to have such a caring stepfather. From the inside, the family was hiding a dark secret. Our biggest concern was the children. When discussing this with Scott and Karen, we asked if they felt that leaving the kids at "grandma's and grandpa's" was best. We asked if it was possible that he might molest their daughter and sons. Karen's response was, "I hope not."

Outsiders do not understand that the family subjected to violence lives in a world dictated by an individual who is self-serving. Outsiders do not understand that in the victim's view, justice brings pain and suffering, truth means humiliation, silence is golden, and wholeness means not being hurt. The victim's self-esteem is not grounded in individual pride; it is grounded in favors and blessings given by a person of power and control. It is not the victim's esteem that matters but the abuser's. The abuser can still control the victim and their family even after the victim has left home!

First, the abuser communicates the *perception of threat* to their family. The family is warned that a system of honor exists that members must uphold. This honor centers on the abuser and is interpreted through him. Truth telling and honesty are only acceptable within the context of the dysfunctional family. Family members are to be honest with one another, but outsiders are not trusted because they bring a sense of threat. Withholding information, covering up, and manipulating others are seen as noble qualities in each member because they protect the honor and secrecy of the family.

> The shame-bound family has many ways to keep the feelings of unworthiness in place. It's not that family members consciously want to feel ashamed, but the feelings of shame keep the secrets secret. The shame keeps one bound to the family out of loyalty, by not talking about what goes on or by playing a role like the joker or the fix-it person. In a family with many generations of unspoken incest, the shame factor keeps each generation tied to the system. A client finds herself ostracized from the family by refusing to let her children go to family events where the males who commit incest will be drinking and partying over the holidays. She faces the family dynamic that in the shame-bound system, even when she is away from the family, the blame falls on her. If she tells the truth, she is punished. She is also discouraged from getting an education or leaving the town in which these generations have perpetuated the lies of incest.[7]

Second, there is a *code of silence*. To communicate with outsiders the truths about the family is taboo. Police, shelter advocates, counselors, school officials, and others present a perceived threat to the stability of the family. The abuser has manipulated the members of the family to believe that outsiders are a threat to the peace and safety of the household. The family members are to reinforce this code by keeping silent or pressuring others to be silent.

7. McClintock, *Sexual Shame*, 24.

To speak out against the sins of the abuser is a violation of the honor of the dysfunctional family. Any member who is not silent will be given the "silent treatment." All other family members are to shun the one who dishonored them by breaking the silence. One woman had kicked her husband out because of his abusive behavior and alcoholism, and his family supported her in this. Once the man went to rehabilitation and said he was sorry, they began to pressure her to take him back. She felt he hadn't changed, but they felt she should take him back anyway. As she resisted, they began to ignore her and to distance themselves from her and the children emotionally and physically.

Third, *fear and humiliation* control the members of the family. Victims and their children fear rejection or punishment from the abuser and other family members. Those who break the rules are humiliated and shamed into submission. Even those who enter the family by marriage are expected to keep the secrets intact. Sometimes an outsider is brought into the system only to be manipulated by the family. The son-in-law keeps quiet because he believes that otherwise he will lose his children, and his wife may divorce him for breaking the silence. The daughter-in-law may see that the son acts like his father but believes she is powerless to do anything.

This dysfunctional family system is dangerous and harmful to the members existing within it. Healthy families empower the members to grow, develop, and mature. Empowering involves faith, trust, respect, love, and encouragement for the benefit of others. The dysfunctional family system does not encourage family members to be what they can be—it encourages them to be what the person in power and control wants them to be. The healthy family cannot be open and live freely within the culture of the dysfunctional family system. The abuser extinguishes the motivation within the family to change, because change can be dangerous to this family system.

Dysfunction, Abuse, and Family Members

How does the abusive family system affect the members of the family? It is important that outsiders who attempt to intervene understand how complex this system is, and how difficult it is for the family to achieve change and true wholeness. It is also important for outsiders to understand why those inside the system must be silent.

Victims

First, victims struggle with a *code of silence*. They are afraid to speak out. They fear punishment through further abuse, neglect, isolation, or humiliation.

They also are concerned about confidentiality. This not only includes keeping what they say confidential but also acting as if one is not aware that the abuser is controlling the family. Victims are expected to keep silent in order to maintain the harmony and integrity of the abuser and family. Women who have been abused share with me that they believe no one will understand them, that they are powerless, and that they are completely dependent on the abusive partner.

Second, victims struggle with *self-respect*. Studies have been done concerning the Stockholm Syndrome.[8] This syndrome creates a type of traumatic bonding that can occur between a victim and an oppressor. When separated from the abuser, the victim and children can sense guilt and a longing for the abuser. Victims are told that their sense of self-worth, love, and respect comes from the abuser. When separated, they experience isolation, guilt, and loneliness. The abuser has conditioned them to depend upon him. An example of this can be found in the story of the Israelite exodus from Egypt. Yahweh brought the Israelites out of slavery, yet after a short while they had a strong desire to return to Egypt. The Israelites had become dependent upon the brutal Pharaoh to the point that they were afraid to trust another leader.[9]

Third, *victims need to be empowered* to develop healthy relationships, characterized by appropriate levels of self-disclosure. I find that many who have suffered abuse or trauma tend to have either strong barriers against self-disclosure or no barriers at all to self-disclosure. This happens due to the codependency and trust issues. We help abuse survivors see human relationships like a yard surrounding a home. In the beginning, they may want to put up a privacy fence or brick wall. As time progresses, and they begin to trust their neighbors, they may use a chain link fence. They should always have a gate, the type of which depends on their comfort zone. Whenever they are hurt, they can close the gate. The idea is that they choose their own fence and can protect their own personal space.

Victims need to be empowered and patiently guided out of abuse. In cases of extreme violence, whether there is a threat to the victim's and to her children's safety, we must work with our legal system to protect the families. Victims must be encouraged to speak out against abuse in their lives. They can be encouraged to listen to that inner voice that they have been told to

8. Dugan and Hock, *It's My Life Now*, 15. This study was performed on victims who were held captive during a bank robbery in Stockholm, Sweden. After the victims were freed, they tended to display a dependence upon their captors a few days after they were released. This dependence was an emotional bond called traumatic bonding.

9. To read more about the Israelites' exodus from Egypt as parallel with families living under domestic violence, see Clark, "Open Your Eyes," 27–36.

ignore and silence. They can be empowered to stand and leave the situation and to provide for themselves and for their children. They can be encouraged to know that God loves them, and that a community will accept them. Acceptance means that the community needs to patiently work by providing them with opportunities for small victories to strengthen them enough to one day confront their abuser. Providing for themselves, training in a vocation, and having a stable home are great victories for those leaving an abusive relationship.

Abusers

Abusers struggle with *control and manipulation* in the family system. They underfunction and expect others to overfunction. This can bring a sense of shame and humiliation. While drugs and alcohol have been blamed for much domestic violence today, these substances often anesthetize the abuser to the pain he feels about being abusive. The abuser may feel guilty about his behavior and try to escape by using alcohol or drugs. Abuse is about power and control, and the abuser uses control to get results. Abusers choose to control others. The community of faith has an opportunity to challenge the abuser to serve others rather than to control them. In the past, this concept of service and self-sacrifice had been placed upon the victims rather than the abusers. However, it is the abuser who must be challenged to serve and repent in order to heal. There must be a balance of power, and many times victims need help in the power struggle.

Second, abusers are struggling with a *lack or fear of intimacy*. They seek to control others because they struggle with low self-esteem. While this combination of narcissism and low self-esteem may seem odd, it demonstrates that abusers feel a need to be praised and loved. They control others because they need others in their lives. They feel that it is important to be praised because they fear rejection. They feel that intimacy has to be forced because they are not comfortable with themselves. Most of the men I have helped have few if any male friends. Those with high anxiety and fears of isolation usually have difficulty differentiating themselves from their emotions.[10] They fear intimacy because they fear being alone. They control others because they need to feel good about themselves. They are narcissistic and seek their own praise over the praise of God.

Churches must not only call abusers to accountability, they must also love them and help them develop spiritually. This does not mean that church

10. Richardson, *Creating a Healthier Church*, 58–59, 63, 86–87.

leaders or members allow themselves to be manipulated. Neither does it mean that churches provide marriage counseling between abuser and victim. Churches must take hold of these men and stand by them. Just as God called a violent man by the name of Saul of Tarsus to accountability, so the church must confront and arrange an encounter with abusers. Just as Barnabas accepted Saul even though the apostles hesitated, so the church must offer hope and spiritual reconciliation to abusers. Just as Saul suffered for and became an advocate for those who had been his victims, so abusers must face the emotional suffering of repentance, reciprocity, and accountability with those whom they have victimized. Their repentance is not lip service—it is a life of service and sacrifice.

Intervention

First, intervention involves *understanding and respecting the cultural and family values that the family presents*. The family must see that the outsider is trying to help rather than hurt the family. Second, intervention involves *empowering the family members to change*. Trying to rescue a victim may only further manipulate her and cause increased guilt. Often an outsider gets an adrenaline rush persuading a woman to leave an abusive relationship. This does not empower the woman—it controls them. This is why it is important for the woman to be supported rather than controlled by outsiders. *The woman should leave only when she is ready*. A common statistic given at abuse workshops suggests that an abused woman leaves and returns to her partner an average of seven times before finally ending the relationship. Whether this is accurate or not, it illustrates that women commonly leave and return more than once. Those who are victims of abuse must be encouraged to become independent and confront their abuser. This may take years of patience, and it involves various stages. The victim must be empowered to heal by accepting that she is precious in God's sight and is worthy of love and respect. She must love herself enough to expect to be loved. We cannot love a neighbor unless we love ourselves.

> Equally important is the need for watchful and supportive relationships with the batterers who feel that they are being abandoned one more time. When a woman leaves her abusive partner, the church community should have a group of men and women, trained in the dynamics of intimate violence, who will, for example, stop by to have lunch or dinner with the man. It is important to encourage the man not to stalk his ex-partner. If the man feels that he has other people who care about his well-being and understand the difficulty of losing his partner

and children, he may be more likely to succeed in his journey toward nonviolence. The church community has a primary responsibility to assure the batterer that he remains connected to a caring community of support.[11]

Abusers must complete the treatment programs required by their state in order to heal and break the cycle of violence and high anxiety that dominates their behavior. Programs are tough and challenging, and individuals will only complete the sessions if they desire to change. Effective programs may involve months or even an entire year of attendance for an abuser to experience change. Batterer-intervention programs are most effective if a combination of confrontation, accountability, and support is used. The spiritual community can also provide support, to form a system of encouragement and accountability for the abuser.

Outsiders must love the abuser enough to hold him accountable for his acts of violence and humiliation. While some would prefer to respond to violent men with violence, this will not prompt change in the violent man. To act with compassion and firmness is an attempt to understand why the abuser behaves as he does.

I sat in the hospital room and visited with Vernon. He was recovering from surgery, and it looked as if the cancer was continuing to grow. He was a man in his sixties who had been estranged from church. My first visit with him and his wife was a few years previous. My wife and I had decided to visit all former members of the church I had begun to preach in this small Missouri town in order to encourage them to return to the congregation. We had been in town two months and were excited to make a difference. Vernon always had a reason why he was not at church that had to do with his unfair treatment from the congregation.

His son, Mike, was also in the room. Mike was a man I had disliked for a year. I had helped Sharon, his wife, leave him, and our church had encouraged her and the kids to leave and be safe. He blamed his abusive behavior on alcohol, on unemployment, and on Sharon. He manipulated me into letting him see Sharon, and I thought he was going to kill her. I vowed never to allow myself to trust him. He was charming and manipulative—just as I had learned in the abuse trainings. He always claimed to be the victim, and now I had to sit in the same room with him.

Mike was silent while Vernon and I spoke. "Good," I thought. "He probably ought to be ashamed of what he did to his family, God, and, of course, me." It was a struggle to smile at him and act cordial. I thought of the conversations

11. Livingston, *Healing Violent Men*, 23.

I had had with his children at church camp, and how he had treated them and their mom.

At least I could talk to Vernon. He knew what Mike was like. It seemed that every statement Vernon made was prefaced with, "Now Ron, you and I understand spiritual matters but, Mike, you won't understand this . . ." Or "Mike, you probably can't relate to this because you don't care about God . . ." Over and over again I heard Vernon bring up Mike's failures, faults, and sins. Mike was "stupid," was "insensitive," or "lacked true knowledge." I began to wonder how Vernon, who was equally as sinful, could be so hard on his son. This was his flesh and blood. Who could Mike turn to for help? In fact, wasn't Vernon a little responsible for how his son sees life, the world, and even God? Yet Mike sat there with his head down and said nothing.

As I left, my heart ached for Mike. I realized I had made an emotional connection with a man I had vowed to hate. I realized that maybe God was teaching me that all humans need love and compassion.

Abusers can be empowered to change if they have a group that accepts them and holds them accountable for their actions. Court-mandated batterer intervention is most effective, but it can also be coupled with church-mandated spiritual growth. The faith community has the authority to require abusers to attend counseling and to meet for spiritual accountability. I have set up regular meetings and prayer sessions with abusive men and have seen a change in their spirituality. I have found them willing to give me permission to contact their batter-intervention leader, parole officer, or other counselor in order to form a network of support and accountability. As with all ministries, this involves risk and trust, as does agape love. It also involves the realization that had I been reared in a dysfunctional family, I too could easily have become abusive and controlling.

Empowering families of domestic violence involves *balancing power in the relationships*. Healthy relationships are about shared power. Relationships should not manipulate, humiliate, or control, or to allow a spouse to do so Intimate-partner relationships should never include a caretaking role (except in cases of severe physical or mental trauma or in the age-related illness of a spouse). Partners should share power and respect each other's rights and dignity. Being a good husband involves empowering his wife to be the best she can be, and being a good wife means empowering her husband to be the best he can be. Marriage is about both spouses fulfilling their responsibilities. This is the meaning of love and honor in a marriage. Partners are not to try to gain power but to empower each other in order to work as a team.

The Community of Faith

In domestic violence, one person has attempted to control, or has gained control over, another. The more powerful one has done this not to better the other person but to better himself. This control smacks of selfishness. It is grounded in conceit rather than in love and empowerment. The victim becomes the one who is controlled and manipulated and begins to see only the needs of the other rather than her own needs. Unfortunately, Christianity's overemphasis on self-sacrifice becomes a tool guiding the behavior of the abuser to further control the other partner. Brian Gill-Austern writes that an unhealthy focus on self-sacrifice and self-denial has the following negative effects on women:[12]

- Self-sacrifice can cause women to lose touch with their own needs and desires.

- Self-sacrifice can lead women to lose a sense of self and a voice.

- Self-sacrifice can create a reservoir of resentment in victimized women.

- Self-sacrifice can lead women to overfunction on behalf of others and to underfunction on behalf of self, which contributes to a loss of both self-esteem and personal direction.

- Self-sacrifice can undermine the capacity of women for genuine mutuality and intimacy.

- Self-sacrifice can create stress and strain.

- Self-sacrifice can lead women to abdicate their responsibility to use their God-given gifts in God's service.

- Self-sacrifice can contribute to exploitation and domination of women's relationships by more powerful parties.

When victims hear sermons, songs, or classes on emptying themselves, they apply this teaching to themselves. They begin to feel guilty if they have not been what God has called them to be. Since self-blame is a natural defense for abuse victims, they feel guilty, as if it is their fault that the marriage suffers.

Faith communities have a great opportunity to help families caught in domestic violence. This begins with the willingness to accept all people and help them to heal. Faith communities must also support, protect, and empower the family. This will demand patience and understanding. Understanding that victims have played a role in an emotional system will be valuable in

---

12. Gill-Austern, "Love Understood as Self-Sacrifice and Self-Denial," 310–15.

guiding them to be strong and confident in their faith. Validating their pain and suffering is necessary for them to grow in Christ. The community of faith must validate their suffering by letting them know that what has happened to them is wrong and unjust. Faith communities must also help restore justice by empowering victims to be safe from their abusers and by advising them on any necessary, protective legal action. Finally, by confessing that they have been abusive, that they have sinned, and that they will do whatever it takes to change and give back to their intimate partners, abusers also must ultimately validate their victims in the context of a faith community. When Moses told the Israelites that God knew their pain, they worshipped Yahweh (Exod 4:16). Just as the Israelites worshiped freely once God had heard them, so victims of domestic violence cannot truly be free until they are validated and able to confront their abusers.

Jesus taught that victims must be able to confront abusers in order for the relationship to be healed (Matthew 18). God is relational and confronts God's children when they sin. Why? God wants relationships to be restored. God wants to be respected and honored. I believe that victims cannot truly heal until they are able to confront their abuser or the memory of their deceased abuser. I will address this in chapter 9.

Unlike victims, abusers cannot see the needs of their spouse because they are focused on their own needs. An abuser believes that his wife has been insubordinate, and that she is the cause of stress in the marriage. This relationship then becomes one of humiliation, and the wife is reprimanded for thinking of herself. She is to be giving and serving, much like the horse in George Orwell's *Animal Farm*. The hard-working servant (the horse) never questions the leaders and ends up in the slaughterhouse, because he needs to be cared for. I am careful about the marriage literature I encourage dysfunctional and abusive families to read. "For better or worse" does not include abuse. "Making lemonade out of lemons" does not sanctify dysfunction and sin. "Blooming where you are planted" does not justify living in an abusive relationship.

Spouses are to support, strengthen, and encourage each other. This involves romance, honesty, forgiveness, accountability, and confronting wrong behavior. Each should feel comfortable holding the other to standards of holiness and honor within the family. This creates a respect between two people who are in a balanced relationship. If there is an imbalance of power, the victim must be protected immediately. God is a God who hears the cries of the victims, and who demands that they be protected. Victims first must be encouraged to be safe, and then the process that strengthens them to confront abuse can begin.

I do not believe that people will truly heal until they can stand against those who have hurt them. When victims are safe, they can begin the process of looking within themselves and discerning that they are to be loved and treated with respect. Because victims have been manipulated or humiliated, many have learned to mistrust anything that makes them feel worthy, especially when it comes from outsiders. They will do what pleases others before they will do what makes themselves happy. They will put themselves at risk in order to serve others. Churches should be aware of this and help them heal by loving, supporting, and listening to their voices.

When the relationship is unbalanced, the abuser also needs to be held accountable for his actions and selfish attitudes. The community of faith can work with trained professionals to provide a safe place for abusers to heal and learn to practice shared power in their relationships.

> The most productive strategy is for churches to work together with other social service providers to support the existing batterer's treatment program. I believe that every community should recognize the importance of reconciling the violent offenders in its midst to the larger community, but this goal is only possible with an extended and rigorous program of responsibility. Where there is already a batterers' treatment program working within the community, the ecclesial community should be sure that part of the process of satisfaction involves attending these meetings.[13]

The community of faith can promote shared power within couples. The church has the right and responsibility to empower victims to heal and to confront those who violate them. Churches that help victims set healthy relational boundaries give them the chance to feel a sense of power. The community must call abusers to submission, accountability, and self-control. When Jesus healed the demon-possessed man (Luke 8:26–39), Jesus did not allow the man to accompany him until the healed man had returned to his community and told them about God. What reaction would this man have faced when walking into the town? People would have remembered him as the "crazy flasher," the violent man, and the howling maniac that could not be controlled. Yet his task was to face those he had hurt and tell them about, as well as show them, his transformation through Jesus.

Likewise, abusers should be called to face those that they have hurt and to hear their pain and cries. In order to heal, abusers have to acknowledge their sinfulness and the effects that their abuse has had on others. The faith community has an opportunity to send abusers back into their community to

13. Livingston, *Healing Violent Men*, 83.

heal, and a great opportunity to allow others to heal as well. The faith community also has the responsibility to protect and validate victims so that they can see that they are made in God's image and worthy of love and respect.

The community of faith can also prevent abuse by teaching men to model the nature of God. Men's classes and fellowships can keep men in accountable relationships with other men. Abusive men usually do not have many male friends. Men's groups can hold them accountable and provide opportunities to develop friendships that many men tend to resist. We in the faith community must also redefine masculinity by the nature of Yahweh, Jesus, and the Holy Spirit. Masculinity is not as narrowly defined as in our culture, but rather it is as diverse as God. God *is one* and practices behavior that is valid for both males and females. Masculinity is not seen in opposition to femininity. Masculinity complements femininity.

Churches can focus on identifying power and control issues in marriage classes, premarital counseling, and youth groups. Family classes can help families develop healthy relationship skills. Youth ministers can work with teens to address dating violence, family violence, and the need to hold one another accountable for abusive behavior.

Domestic violence affects everyone. But does everyone affect domestic violence? Even more than this, do the people of God become as involved as their Lord in addressing domestic violence?

CHAPTER 4

How Does God Feel
about Abuse?

What Is Theology?

T HEOLOGY CAN BE a frightening word. It seems that when we hear *theology* we think of something abstract, something distant from common concerns, or an academic exercise. Many people seem apprehensive about theology, but it is meant to make a complex message about God relevant to people. When Jesus spoke in parables, he was practicing theology. When the Apostle Paul explained Jewish texts to common Gentiles, he was practicing theology. When the writers of Proverbs made life applications drawing on common experience, from tending animals to living through daily events, they were practicing theology. When the prophets spoke God's message in metaphors and stories, they were practicing theology.

A Study or Discussion about God

Theology means "a study or discussion about God."[1] While Christians have many issues, discussions, and doctrines that can exhaust their time, these issues are futile if they do not begin with a discussion about God. Whenever we are asked, "What does God have to say about . . . ?" or "What does the Bible say about . . . ?" we are being forced to begin with God. God is our authority, and the nature, actions, and heart of God are where we begin.

Human Discussion and Interaction

Second, theology *involves human discussion and interaction*. A study that begins with God must eventually extend to human beings. We call this *theological*

---

1. The word *theology* comes from two Greek words: *Theos* means "God" and *logos* means "word" or "study." A simple definition of *theology* is "the study of God" or "the sharing of words about God."

reflection. Theological reflection is not an individual process; it is a group process. Once we learn something about God, we must share what we have learned. While Western culture is very individualistic, Eastern culture has a desire to dialogue, discuss, share, and learn with or from others. Western people tend to individually reflect on what they have learned. Eastern people tend to share ideas and look for a consensus. Since the biblical culture came from the ancient Near Eastern world, it seems logical that theological reflection, dialogue, and consensus are part of the Judeo-Christian culture.

> With no direction/guidance the people fall but there is safety with many advisors. (Prov 11:14)

> The way of a fool seems correct in their eyes but a wise person listens to advice. (Prov 12:15)

> Plans fail for lack of counsel, but with many advisers they succeed. (Prov 15:22)

An Articulation of Faith

Finally, theology is an *articulation of a faith that seeks to learn*.[2] As we seek to know more about God, and we discuss and reflect upon our understanding with others, it is important that we can state what we believe. Theology has a purpose in mind. It is to be a guide to help people draw closer to the Creator and to better understand the nature and heart of God. We study to learn, dialogue to reflect, and share to inform others about this God. Much of the work in domestic-violence prevention involves becoming aware of and discussing God's view of victims and abusers. While a study of God leads to a conviction, the practice of theology can develop relationships with others and strengthen this *faith seeking understanding*. Thus it is important to speak with victims or abusers about God and domestic violence.

Christian theology suggests that God is revealed in nature, Scripture, and the words and actions of Jesus Christ. While nature cannot reveal the personal character of God, Jesus reveals how God feels about children, women, the oppressed, and humanity.[3] Jesus is the reflection of God, representing the nature and heart of the Creator for all humans (Col 1:15; Hebrews 1–2). Jesus's ministry is the model for our obedience to God and our practicing the works of God.

2. Grenz, *Theology for the Community of God*, 1.
3. Erickson, *Christian Theology*, 715; Grenz, *Theology for the Community of God*, 245.

> Even though he was a son he learned obedience from what he suffered
> and when he finished, all of those who obey him have a way for eternal
> salvation. (Heb 5:18)

The Spirit also reflects the nature and heart of God. God has placed the Spirit within humans not only as a testimony to God's existence but as a source of power to help Christians become like Jesus.

> When the encourager comes, whom I send from the Father, the Spirit
> of truth, which goes from the Father, that one will testify about me.
> (John 15:26)

> Those who live according to the sinful nature think fleshly but those
> who live according to the Spirit are spiritual. To think fleshly brings
> death but to think spiritually brings life and peace. Therefore to think
> fleshly makes one an enemy of God, because they are not able and can-
> not submit to the law of God. They are not able to and cannot please
> God. But you are not fleshly! You are spiritual, since the Spirit of God
> lives in you. (Rom 8:5–9)

Theology and Domestic Violence: God's Nature and Abuse

How does God feel about victims and batterers? What does the Bible teach about domestic violence and the nature of God's people? Are power and control characteristics of God? When batterer-intervention providers or victims' advocates talk, a discussion about God usually tends to focus on the book of Joshua and the violent wars of the Old Testament.[4] While the Old Testament presents these as issues of violence, power, and control, this only represents one angle on the nature of God. We must acknowledge that God does punish and allows the use of violence on individuals and nations that continually re-sist the Creator. We must also remember that God warned the people of Israel to repent for decades and sometimes centuries before enacting punishment. It is fair to believe that this represents a small portion of God's actions.

Overwhelmingly, *God practices mercy, forgiveness, and patience.* Violence is usually a final act after years, decades, or centuries of patience. In Exodus 34:6–7, God was revealed as one who is "compassionate, gracious, slow to anger, abounding in love and faithfulness, maintaining love to thousands, and forgiving wickedness, rebellion, and sin." God punishes the wicked for three or four generations, but extends forgiveness to a thousand generations

---

4. I usually try to avoid the terms "Old Testament" and "New Testament" by using "Hebrew Scriptures" and "Greek Scriptures" since these terms are more correct. In this book I have chosen to keep the traditional terms since most readers are familiar with this terminology.

(Deut 7:9). Forgiveness, patience, and mercy are major characteristics of God's nature. When God forgave the Ninevites, Jonah replied with, "I knew that you are a gracious and merciful God, slow to anger and full of faithfulness, a God who feels sorry for the evil ones" (Jonah 4:2). In the Old Testament, God is shown as one who forgives an unfaithful wife, renews a covenant with a sinful nation, gives life to a people who will turn away, and enters a covenant with a people, knowing that "their heart is inclined to do evil from their youth" (Gen 8:21). God's nature is not one of violence and anger but one of love, mercy, and compassion. To focus on God's anger is to have a limited perspective of the divine nature. The Bible describes the nature of God as merciful and compassionate.

In the incarnation, the nature of God is seen in Jesus. The gospel writers described Jesus as someone who was meek, was patient, cried, listened to women, held children, and encouraged the oppressed. Early Christian writers described Jesus as patient, loving, and compassionate. The Bible tells us that Jesus is the reflection and image of Yahweh (Col 1:15; Heb 1:4). Yet as the risen Lord, Jesus has put his enemies under his feet (Acts 2:35). Even though the risen Lord acts in vengeance and repays those who do evil, yet we tend to remember him as a forgiving, loving, and compassionate Messiah. Jesus came to explain God's nature and character, not redefine it. He came to show us the compassion, justice, and character of God (John 1:18; Heb 1:3). The Holy Spirit also reflects the nature of God. The Holy Spirit does bring the conviction and judgment of God (Acts 5:1–11), yet it overwhelmingly represents the peace of God.

> But the fruit of the Spirit is love, joy, peace, endurance, kindness, goodness, faithfulness, meekness, and self-control. . . . If we live by the Spirit we must be in order with the Spirit. (Gal 5:22–25)

God's nature is shown in the Scriptures, the incarnation, and the Spirit as one of compassion, peace, and patience.

Power and control are issues that must be addressed concerning the nature of God. Does God control human beings? Are children of God coerced into submission and worship? Do we have free will? Can we make our own choices? Is our future already set? Theology calls us to study the nature of God and to reflect on the divine presence in Jesus and the Spirit. Since God's nature is one of gentleness, mercy, and compassion, then how does God feel about abuse? More important, how does God feel about those who physically, emotionally, verbally, and sexually abuse or humiliate others? If mercy is part of God's nature, then what do we do with power and control? A study of God and domestic violence challenges us to ask these questions and seek answers.

Since God seeks relationship with humans, we can believe that God is relational. In the Garden of Eden, God said that it was not good for the man to be alone (Gen 2:18). Humans are created in God's image or "our image" (Gen 1:26). Just as in English, so in Hebrew the word *our* suggests that God is a plurality or community, as are humans. In the first few centuries of the church, theologians posited that God existed as a Trinity (as Father, Son, and Holy Spirit). God seeks relationship because God exists in relationship and initiates covenant.

Regardless of how wicked, sinful, rebellious, or disobedient humans have proven to be, God continues to call humans to repentance and to maintain a covenant with the creation. In covenant with creation, God proved to be faithful and honorable by meeting human needs. When humans break or transgress the covenant, God is dishonored in the world (Mal 1:6). God then has two options in order to restore or maintain honor in the presence of creation—punishment or forgiveness. Forgiveness is an option, but it involves repentance by the sinner. Punishment is another option, and it involves no action by the transgressor. Therefore God maintains honor by providing for those in the covenant and practicing justice. Humans have the responsibility to honor God by obeying the covenant. God honors us by blessing us and being faithful.[5]

In a covenant relationship exists the possibility of one party's being unfaithful. God *chooses* to uphold the terms of the covenant. God is faithful, cannot lie, and keeps promises (Deut 7:7–9; Titus 1:4). However, humans have *chosen* to be unfaithful to the covenant. At times, God punished transgressors (Isa 54:6; Jer 3:8). Sometimes when sinners prayed, God *chose* not to hear them, as in the case of the people of Judah under Babylonian captivity (Jer 11:9–14; 14:11–12; Ezek 8:18). Most of the time when sinners appealed to God, they were forgiven (Jonah 3:10; 1 Kgs 21:28–29). In every example of interaction, God made a *choice*. Whether it was forgiveness or punishment, God was exercising a *choice*. In every example the people made a *choice*. In covenant there exists *choice*, free will, honor, and mutual respect. God does not force humans into a decision. God gives humans the ability to choose good or evil in the world and while in covenant.

Power and control involve coercion, manipulation, and abuse. God does not engage in relationships in this way. When people continue to choose to

---

5. The English words *faith* and *faithfulness* are each encompassed by a single word in Greek and in Hebrew. The Hebrew *chesed* is usually translated "lovingkindness" but has the meaning of "faithfulness" or "loyalty" when it appears in the context of covenant. God's *chesed* suggests that God is faithful to the covenant. For humans, *chesed* suggests loyalty and obedience in the covenant.

sin, God allows Satan, a ruler, an army, or the events of life to affect them. God does not force people to make a certain choice. God persuades through the preaching by others and pleads for people to choose the truth. Because of this choice, God's method of outreach is not by coercion but by persuasion.

> Stand in the courtyard of Yahweh's house and speak to all the people of the towns of Judah who come to worship in the house of Yahweh. Tell them everything I command you to speak; do not omit a word. Perhaps they will listen and each will turn from their evil way. *Then I will feel sorry and not bring evil on them* because of the evil they have done. (Jer 26:2–3)

> *I do not delight in the death of anyone*, declares the Lord *Yahweh*. Repent and live! (Ezek 18:32)

God empowers those in covenant to see the truth and make right choices. One example of God's help comes from 1 Corinthians 10:13.

> You have not received any temptation except what is common to man. God is faithful and will not permit you be tempted beyond what you are able to do, but with the temptation you will have a way out so that you can bear it.

The passage tells us that God empowers us to overcome sin and temptation. First, God protects us from excessive evil and *does not allow* more than we can handle. The Creator keeps Satan at bay and allows the devil only limited power over individuals (Job 1–2). Second, God still *allows us* to have a choice. We have the potential and ability to choose evil or good, and God knows this. Third, *God has faith that we can make the right choice.* God hopes in us, even though we are weak, and believes that we have the right and ability to resist sin.

God persuades, protects, and empowers us so that we can make a right choice. The fact that we choose evil is not a reflection upon God, but it brings a sense of shame. The shame is not upon us but God. Our choosing evil may grieve God, but it does not discredit the divine nature. God cannot be blamed for the choices of others, yet our choosing that which is good provides a great sense of joy to God. Within covenant there is always the ability to choose good or evil. The choices, not the control, bring honor or shame to God. If God could intervene, humans would not have free will and free choice.[6]

This was evident in Jesus's ministry. Jesus *empowered* the disciples to stand on their own feet and be faithful. The Spirit also *empowers* others by dwelling within them. Yet the Spirit can be quenched (1 Thess 5:18), grieved

---

6. Boyd, *Is God to Blame?* 63.

(Eph 4:29), and is submissive to prophets (1 Cor 14:32). Morally, Christians can live in such a way that they either walk with the Spirit or drive it out. The Spirit *empowers* the people of God to live holy lives, but it does not control or overpower them. This is why preaching and persuading are important tasks in the ministry of Christ and the Spirit.

God does exhibit power over evil. While Satan and evil are allowed to exist, God punishes and judges evil and those who practice it. God is a God of justice, and evil has limited power; but at the end of its time, God wins. Throughout the Bible God displays judgment at various times. Because humans have free choice, they are given the opportunity to choose between good and evil. Yet at God's decided time (usually called *Yom Yahweh* or the "day of the LORD"), judgment happens and the wicked are punished. Pagan nations punish the unfaithful, and those nations that refuse to humble themselves before Yahweh are punished. God allows humans to choose and face the blessings or consequences of those choices. God is a god of justice. God uses force to balance power and vindicate or protect victims. God also confronts those who use power over others.

God also practices vengeance. Solomon Schimmel suggests that many victims suffer because they are told that vengeance or the desire for revenge or justice is wrong. Yet God brings revenge on the wicked through objective institutions. Schimmel indicates that those who are hurt may not be able to dispense proper judgment on their abuser. The purpose of legal systems is to properly weigh out the evidence and the nature of the criminal and to call them to repentance while validating the victim.[7] This is evident in Paul's challenge to let God take care of revenge (Rom 12:19) followed by the statement that authorities are God's agents for punishing evil workers (Rom 13:4). This tells Christians that God will use human institutions to punish those who oppress and victimize others. While this seems violent, it is God's way of providing impartial judgment on criminals.

A third issue concerning the nature of God is the *fate of the oppressed.* God is the defender of the oppressed (Exod 22:22–24; Ps 9:9; Prov 17:5). Oppression makes God angry.

> Do not mistreat a widow or an orphan. If you do and they cry out to me, I will certainly hear their cry. My anger will be aroused, and I will kill you by the sword; your wives will become widows and your children fatherless. (Exod 22:22–24)

7. Schimmel, *Wounds Not Healed by Time*, 21–23.

God commanded the Israelites to protect and defend the oppressed. The oppressed included widows, orphans, the poor, foreigners, and any others who are victims in society.[8] God led the Israelites out of Egypt and protected them because they were oppressed (Exod 22:21). They were also expected to show this same concern for the oppressed. Throughout the Hebrew Scriptures, God became angry when nations abused and oppressed the weak of society. Women, children, and foreigners were in this category. It is God's nature to protect and defend the cause of the weak and oppressed.[9]

> The one who oppresses the poor despises their maker, but whoever is kind to the needy honors God. (Prov 14:31)

> Do not move an ancient boundary stone or encroach on the fields of the orphans for their defender (redeemer or kinsman) is strong and will take up their case against you. (Prov 23:10–11)

Jesus also reflects the nature of God in his ministry. The Gospel of Luke illustrates God's passion for the weak and oppressed. In Luke 4:16–19, Jesus proclaims in the synagogue that his mission involves freeing the captives, helping the blind to see, releasing the oppressed, and preaching good news to the poor.

Jesus shows the same passion for the oppressed that God displayed in the Old Testament. The two judgment scenes in the gospels (Matt 25:31–46; Luke 16:19–31) warn people who had neglected the needs of the poor and oppressed. Jesus condemns and rejects such people. In the book of Acts, the Holy Spirit also displays this compassionate nature. The Spirit sent the early church to the Gentiles, to the poor, to widows, and to outcasts. The Spirit condemned Ananias and Sapphira for lying about the amount of money they had distributed to the poor (Acts 5:1–11) and sent Paul and Barnabas to the Gentiles (Acts 13:1–3, 52). Paul saw this mission as a way to remember the poor (Gal 2:10).

Finally, the nature of God is seen in a *relationship with humanity*. Such a relationship between God and humanity demonstrates God's faithfulness, God's relationality, and God's passion. Covenant became God's means of establishing with humans a relationship grounded in faithfulness. Covenants became major events in the various stages of human history. God made covenants with Noah and with the earth, with Abraham, with David, with the people

8. The Hebrew word for "oppressed" is *'aniy*. This word is translated later by the Greek word *tapeinos*, which is used for "humble." The humble are those humiliated and oppressed in society. Do victims of domestic violence fit into this category?

9. Bennett, *Injustice Made Legal*, 1–2.

of Judah as they returned home from exile, and with the world through Jesus Christ. God has always been the initiator of these covenants. Yet God does not tolerate a dysfunctional relationship in covenant. God does not establish a relationship that ignores sin. God deserves to be respected, honored, loved, and obeyed. God desires a partner who is faithful.

Given that God 's nature is relational, God seeks a healthy, compassionate, and supportive relationship with humans. God's vision for humans entails mutual respect, honor, and blessing. God is not a doormat; but neither is God interested in control, manipulation, or overfunctioning from either covenant partner. God desires to be known, respected, and honored by the creation. Theology (study of God's nature) tells us that God is not a God of wrath and anger but one of peace, mercy, and compassion. God is faithful and chooses to forgive and love human beings.

God's relational nature certainly displays God's own passions. So our relational God grieves, rejoices, and forgives. To risk rejection and joy are powerful characteristics of the nature of God. The very God who initiates love is a God who risks rejection or acceptance.

Indeed, Jesus demonstrated this same passion in his ministry. He wept, drove sinners out of the temple, challenged the disciples, rebuked the Pharisees, held children, encouraged widows and parents of deceased children, and rejoiced. Jesus initiated a relationship with other humans and called the disciples "friends" (John 15:12). Jesus asked Peter, James, and John to accompany him in a time of grief (Mark 14:34), and he watched a friend betray him (Luke 22:61). Jesus became close to other humans so that he could experience the joy of relationship and the pain of betrayal and abuse.

The Spirit, likewise, lives among humans to guide and intercede for them (Rom 8:5–16). Yet a life of sin can grieve or quench the Spirit (1 Thess 5:18; Eph 4:29). A relational God is not a weak God but a passionate one.

Theology tells us that our Creator stands for the weak and is angry when victims are abused or oppressed. Yet God continues to seek healthy relationships with humans. Theology also tells us that God empowers us to choose good. God does not control humans but guides us and believes that we can choose good over evil. So what does theological reflection tell us about God and abuse?

Theological Reflection and Abuse

Domestic-violence ministry's greatest impact on our theology must be that it drives us to the Scriptures. It should cause us to reflect on the nature of God.

Christians must address abuse not just because it is a social-justice issue, but because it is a theological issue. It is not only a crime against humanity, it is a sin against God and those in God's image. It is evil in a world created good.

How did my wife and I come to this conclusion? We began to work with victims' advocates, we went to workshops, and then we began to help victims. Throughout this process, we talked with advocates and counselors and heard their opinions about churches' posture on the problem of domestic violence. Apathy from churches about this issue drives us forward. The bad advice or bad theology that ministers have given women who left their husbands over abuse disturbs me. The more we learned, the more we searched the Scriptures. The more we listened, the more we reflected. The more we faced apathy, the bolder we became.

If the church wants to practice *good theology* concerning domestic violence and abuse, we must dialogue with those who work in abuse prevention and intervention.

> I have also had a few dozen clients over the years who belong to fundamentalist religious groups, usually Christian or Islamic fundamentalist or Orthodox Judaic. Abusive men from these groups tend to openly espouse a system in which women have next to no rights and a man is entitled to be the unquestioned ruler of the home. To make matters worse, these religious sects have greatly increased their political power around the globe over the past two decades . . . Women who live within these religous groups may feel especially trapped by abuse, since their reistance to domination is likely to be viewed as evil and the surrounding community may support or even revere the abuser.[10]

Abuse-intervention advocates consistently indicate a sense of distrust toward churches and ministers. Many abuse victims struggle to believe in a loving and caring God. A high majority of the atheists I have talked with have concerns about believing in God when our world has such a problem with abuse. My wife and I have worked hard to earn their respect and prove to them that we will protect victims of abuse. This has taken much time, energy, and discussion. We sit at the table with victims, abusers, and counselors and talk openly about what we know of God. It is the responsibility of faith communities to draw the oppressed into our sermons, classes, and discussions in order to accurately talk about the nature of God.

The church must deal with social justice because the church is supposed to be the representation of Christ in the world. Domestic violence is an issue that forces us to the Scriptures and causes us to ask questions. Theological

10. Bancroft, *Why Does He Do That?* 166.

reflection from domestic-violence victims, intervention specialists, and batterers themselves is an important resource. If we want to grow in this area, we must invite the oppressed and those who work with the oppressed to the table.

> Many voices declare that the church has either caused men to be violent toward their wives or at least provided fertile soil for men's mistreatment of power within their families. They argue that since the church is part of the problem, it cannot be part of the solution. Thus when violence against women is being discussed, God's people are seldom consulted. Since we speak out so infrequently about violence, our collective voice is never heard on this issue. Generally speaking, leaders in religious organizations and those involved in community pastoral care are never even invited to participate at the secular consultation table. The silence of our churches and our leaders is often interpreted in the public square as complicity with violent acts.[11]

Those who work to prevent abuse will ask questions and challenge us to reflect on and review many of our doctrines. They will send us back to the Scriptures to reexamine many of our traditions and much of our past theology. To dismiss theology's warrant for addressing divorce, dysfunctional-family issues, and abuse is theologically to hide our head in the sand.

This theological relfection on the problem of domestic violence will cause us to rearticulate our faith in a different manner. What issues become important to the Christian community? How do we view hot topics such as marriage, family, divorce, dating, and male-female relationships? How does this attitude of entitlement influence theology constructed by men and women? Suddenly we who are called by God have to take off our rose-colored glasses and see the plight of the oppressed. Our focus on spiritual growth, faith, mercy, and peace must be seen in a new light.

For instance, I have changed my preaching concerning marriage and divorce. My wife and I have also become more effective at leading others through divorce recovery. Our view of healthy families and our family ministry are changing. The empshasis of premarital and marital counseling has changed. When we talk about husbands and wives, we talk about respect and encouragement. Our men's classes and our youth-group teachings are different from what they used to be. People who are rude, verbally abusive, and intimidating are no longer people with *personality quirks*; they are people with *spiritual issues*. Being led by the Spirit has more to do with the way we treat people than with how much Bible we know or how many church services we attend.

---

11. Kroeger and Nason-Clark, *No Place for Abuse*, 16.

The Christian view of evangelism must also change. Evangelism means that the church has a prophetic voice in the community. Evangelism means that we go to the oppressed (Luke 4:16–19) rather than to wait for them to come into the building. If they do come to us, we must believe that God has sent them so that they can receive help. Sometimes evangelism and a prophetic voice are a response we give when we see injustice and are provoked to action. Our church is known in our community by what we stand for, and what we stand against. *The congregation is not a consumer in the community; it is a resource for the community.* We not only minister to our own, we minister to our neighbors and to the world. Evangelism is compassion rather than an intellectual assent to Jesus. Evangelism is love rather than selfishness.

The church cannot hide from the need to exercise compassion and justice in addressing domestic violence. The introduction to this book suggested that the church's failure to address social maladies is a major problem in our country. The church's posture toward issues of domestic violence is not a problem only in the United States but also in other countries. For example, a minister who had been a missionary in Zimbabwe for many decades once lectured that we need to get out of our offices and be in the community. During the question-and-answer session, I asked him how the church was responding to abuse in Zimbabwe.

"We don't have a problem with abuse," he replied.

The statistics concerning abuse in Third-World countries are staggering. How could someone who has lived in such a country say that his area does not have a problem with abuse? Bringing together theology and the problem of domestic violence forces us to open our eyes, to reflect, and articulate an understanding of God for the common person. Our theology and their theology must become one. Why? Because their God and our God must be one!

CHAPTER 5

Is God an
Abuser?

One of our older members shared with me that her father, Marvin, was pretty cruel to her mother, Mildred, while they were growing up. When Mildred was a single young woman she provided childcare for a family. A husband and wife, Charles and Mary, had hired her to care for their children. Things seemed to work well for a while. After months of employment, Charles became attracted to Mildred and forced himself on her. She became pregnant, and to save the family honor, Charles's younger brother, Marvin, was coerced into marrying her. Marvin neglected the firstborn son, Randolph. Even though Randolph grew up thinking that Marvin was his father, he struggled with the pain and rejection he felt from Marvin. More children were born to this marriage, including the woman telling me the story. She shared with me that her dad was a bitter man and cruel to Mildred, yet they went to church faithfully and were involved in many church activities. Mildred died, and eventually so did Marvin. When the children were going through his possessions, they found out about the parentage of the oldest son, Randolph. He had suffered emotional scars because of the bitterness of his supposed "father" Marvin. Marvin's cruelty to Mildred also affected the family. The woman telling me the story told me that, after the funeral, the adult children found many religious books in Marvin's library. What I heard next sent chills down my spine. "Ron," she said, "in dad's books he had highlighted every passage that talked about women submitting to their husbands or that women were to be obedient." She then said, "He never highlighted the passages or commentaries about men and about being a good husband and father. How could a man be that cruel and go to church?"

MALE PRIVILEGE IS the attitude that men have a right to demand honor, respect, and submission from women and children. Male privilege suggests that men rule and women say, "Yes, sir!" Male privilege is seen on *The Honeymooners* when Jackie Gleason would threaten to hit his wife, Alice, and send her "to the moon!" Male privilege is shown when Archie Bunker calls his wife a "dingbat," and when Edith seems to crave this type of attention. Male privilege is seen when rock musicians have scantily clad women sexually and erotically bowing. Male privilege exists when pornographic magazines, websites, media, and advertisements suggest that women should be seen as sex objects *for* men. Male privilege happens when men degrade women for money, attention, or publicity. Male privilege suggests that women need to be "good girls" in order to attract a man, and that maternity gives a woman worth.[1] Male privilege does not always originate with men; women can also encourage it. Women who turn their heads from incidents of male privilege or allow their sons to abuse are pushing the male-privilege agenda.

A movie that illustrates this battle among women is *The Color Purple*. In the movie, the mother, played by Whoopi Goldberg, encourages her son to beat his "strong-willed wife," played by Oprah Winfrey. Goldberg's character is an abused wife, and she feels that this is good advice for her son. Later, an angry Winfrey comes to confront her mother-in-law and indicates that she had given her son the wrong advice (both Winfrey and her movie husband have black eyes as a result of abuse). This is an excellent illustration of how women have become a part of the male-privilege problem in America. Winfrey, the strong woman, would not allow herself to be disrespected. Goldberg's character, through time, became an equally strong woman and left her abusive husband, played by Danny Glover. *The Color Purple* communicates a message that Jackson Katz has stated often: "Strong men are attracted to strong women; weak men are intimidated by strong women."[2]

God, however, does not practice male privilege. Humans submit and humble themselves to God because we realize that only God can handle the tasks ahead. However, God does not force our submission. As the Creator, God is willing to lead those who wish to submit and fight the battle between good and evil. Creator privilege is not based on fear or control; it is based on respect, love, and a willingness to yield. God calls for willing submission and obedience rather than forced respect. While this seems manipulative to some, we must remember that God always initiates covenant, promises to be faithful, and carries the burden of the relationship.

> For when I brought your fathers out of Egypt I did not just give them commands about burnt offerings and sacrifices, but I gave them this command: I said, "Obey me, and I will be your God and you will be my people. Walk in all the ways I command you, so that it may go well with you." (Jer 7:22–23)

1. Mananzan, "Feminine Socialization, 47–49.
2. Katz, "More Than a Few Good Men."

The responsibilities of the weaker client party in ancient Near Eastern covenants were to support, respect, and submit. While this seems offensive to most Americans, it is still a part of life in other countries. The strong are expected to help the weak. In our country we do practice this, although we call it a donation or a tax write-off. Wealthy businesses support sports teams, community projects, and environmental issues. Employers give raises, insurance, or vacations to employees. Schools give retirements to teachers and offer sports programs that do not always benefit the school financially but do provide recreation for students. When employees face financial difficulties, we call upon the business to carry the financial burden for their "clients." Why? Deep down we believe that those who have should provide for those who need help. Yet we as clients also see our responsibility to support these institutions and provide them with a sense of loyalty and security.

This is an example of covenant. Both parties work together to bless or mutually benefit each other. Can this covenant or patron-client relationship be misused? Yes. Both sides can misuse the relationship. We see this when the employee treats his job and company only as a "stepping stone," or when the company fires the longtime employee because she is a "liability." We see this when the company leaders embezzle money, and the employees lose their retirement benefits. We see this when the company closes because of employee theft. We see this often and yet forget that the relationship is not the problem, nor is the patron the one we should fear. The relationship between greater and lesser is not always wrong. It is the *misuse* of that relationship that is wrong. An evil heart can damage many people. When the patron provides for us, we support, serve, respect, and sometimes submit. We have no problem entering a contract with those who help us and wish to act in our best interest.

Male privilege, however, *expects* and *demands* submission from equals. Creator privilege *earns* respect and willing submission. Male privilege uses *manipulation and coercion* to gain power over a wife or female partner and over those the male sees as weaker. Creator privilege *seeks to persuade and empower* humans to work with God to fight evil. Male privilege is driven by *fear and insecurity*. Creator privilege acts out of *love, compassion, and mercy*. Creator privilege also carries greater responsibility to *empower and provide for others*. Male privilege only *takes from others*.

Marriage is about shared power within a covenant relationship. In counseling others, I have rarely met a woman who is not willing to support her husband emotionally as provider for the family, even if it means staying home with the children. I also find more husbands willing to stay home with the children if they know that their wives are able to provide a better income for the family. I see that husbands and wives can work together in a covenant relationship, where one carries the financial burden, and the other supports and respects the spouse for that sacrifice. Yet I feel it is equally important for the working spouse to validate the spouse who takes responsibility for child care and house maintenance. In a healthy marriage, spouses work together to provide for the financial and emotional needs of the family. I find that many women "submit" to their husbands because they choose to, not because they are forced. I also find that many husbands equally respect and "submit" to their wives in decisions and issues within the family. This type of relationship practices shared power and mutual respect. It means acting as a team.

God the Father/ Husband

I have attempted to be sensitive to the use of gender language in my description of God throughout this book. Jesus's statement "God is Spirit," suggests to me that God is neither male nor female (John 4:24). Both males and females are created in God's image (Gen 1:27–28). Yet Israel, like its neighbors, continually tried to worship male and female deities (Jer 44:19). The Assyrian goddess Asherah was placed next to Yahweh (2 Kgs 23:13; Ezek 8:5) in their cities and places of worship. The ancient world needed to distinguish male and female natures in their theology, but Yahweh claimed to be warrior, father, mother, and gentle healer (Isa 66:13).[3] Yahweh was neither male nor female, and both genders can reflect God's nature.

Jesus, according to Greco-Roman culture, also exhibited male and female behaviors in his ministry. His emphasis on mercy, compassion, and peace; the presence of women and children in his ministry; and the choice to be single would have all been suspect to male honor in the ancient world. This does not suggest that we respond by calling God "she" or overemphasize the biblical images of masculinity describing God and the Spirit. We should understand that God is spirit, and that men and women reflect God's nature. But male references about God, Jesus, and the Spirit send an important message to men.

First, the revelation of God in Scripture is meant to *teach us something about the divine nature.* When God was revealed in the Bible, it suggests that something new was being taught. God intervenes in time and space to teach humans and to get their attention. Second, God's being understood as male in biblical cultures *suggests to men something different.* What was the message that God revealed? In the Scriptures, God was showing men how they should behave. It seems that men have proven to be a problem in the history of God's

---

3. Yahweh also claims to "beget" or give birth to the children of Israel (Isa 66:9, 13).

world. The sins of adultery, idolatry, drunkenness, violence, and social injustice; the sins of oppressing widows, orphans, and aliens; and the sins of
poor leadership were problems for Israel. While we have stories of sinful
females in the Scriptures, the majority of stories involve men disobeying God
and being violent to others. In the stories of Scripture, God was trying to teach
men how to submit and how to act in their community. This is why there is
such an emphasis on the mercy, compassion, peace, forgiveness, and love of
God in the Bible. God was identifying the "new-world man." What God was
saying is, "Men, this is how you should act!" In fact it seems to have been the
women and children who understood submission, loyalty, and faithfulness
better than the men.

God's Revelation in a Dysfunctional Culture

By the time Jesus came to earth, the family and society of Palestine were undergoing tremendous change. The Jews were scattered throughout the Roman
Empire. The development of a unified world culture (which Alexander the
Great called the *oikomenē*) and the increase in divorce and blended families
had an impact on how individuals saw themselves in the world. People in
the Greco-Roman culture began to desire salvation, monotheism, associations and clubs, and a sense of connectedness to their world, spirituality, and
each other.[4] They longed for family connections, which clubs, synagogues,
and congregations provided.[5] Christianity's emphasis on family terms such
as *home, called out* (the term for "church" [*ekklēsia*]), *chosen, brothers* and
sisters, father, fellowship, and *children* was a response to experiences sought
by people of the time. Paul's use of the verb *katallassō* ("to reconcile") and his
introduction of a compound form of this verb—*apokatallaso*—suggest that
Paul turned a popular Greek word into a common Christian term.[6] This reconciliation and the family were important truths that God and Christianity
supplied to a lonely world in the first century. The world that received the
incarnation longed to have the hearts of the fathers turned to the children
and each other.

Jesus's use of "Father" and "Son" terminology to describe his relationship
with God suggests that he was modeling a relationship needed in the ancient
world. His use of the Aramaic word *abba* with God the Father also suggests

---

4. Tripolitis, *Religions of the Hellenistic Roman Age*, 2, 6.

5. Hellerman, *The Ancient Church as Family*, 3-4; Harland, *Associations, Synagogues, and Congregations*, 29.

6. Porter, *"Katallasso" in Ancient Greek Literature*, 16.

that he was revealing a relationship that people desired from their God. While the Jewish culture used the family as a vehicle for seeing God, the church used the family to illustrate a loving God in a dysfunctional-family society, that is, in a society where what we today would call dysfunctional families were common. Rather than view God through the family, the early church sought to redefine the family through God and Jesus..

> Here are my mother and my brothers! Whoever does the will of God is my brother and sister and mother. (Mark 3:34–35)

> Husbands, love your wives just as Christ loved the church . . . (Eph 5:25)

> As apostles of Christ we could have been a burden to you, but we were gentle among you, like a nurse caring for her little children . . . For you know that we dealt with each of you as a father deals with his own children, encouraging, comforting, and urging you to live lives worthy of God, who calls you into his kingdom and glory. (1 Thess 2:6–7, 11–12)

God and the ministry of the church were the models for the family. In a dysfunctional family system, the place to begin was God. Therefore, the church called people out of their dysfunctional families into a new family. The church also called fathers and husbands to a new model of family and marriage.

The Dysfunctional-Family World in the First Century

Recent studies on the Roman family have provided valuable information concerning the roles of fathers in the development and leadership of the home. Fathers had complete power over their children, and this has led today's interpreters to view the family head as harsh and cruel. The view of the Roman father as cruel and abusive has been drawn from texts that speak out against the abuse of children, but these texts do not necessarily indicate that most parents practiced this abusive behavior. There was, however, an attitude of indifference rather than harshness toward children. Children were treated better than slaves, but the high infant mortality rate and indifference toward small children indicates that children were not treated as well as they are in modern times. It seems that in upper-class families, fathers played more of a delegating role and entrusted the major tasks of child development to slaves, schools, and sometimes to their wives. While some fathers were concerned about the development of their children, the majority of the child-rearing work was done by others.

Christian marriage and parenting, however, involved compassion (Luke 11:1–12) and gentleness (Col 3:21). Husbands were to love and to initiate faithfulness to their wives (Eph 5:33–47). Fathers, rather than the *pedagogues*, were to discipline and instruct their own children. Fathers were also challenged to train their children by nurturing them in the instruction and warning of the Lord as part of the Christian household, rather than delegating it to child minders and wet nurses (Eph 6:4). Paul called fathers to be involved in disciplining, instructing, and nurturing their children (1 Thess 2:10–12). *One way that Christianity brought a sense of stability, love, and compassion to the family was through male spiritual leadership.*

Male Privilege or Male Modeling

The biblical texts do not give men permission to command, expect, or force respect and submission from females and children in the community. The use of masculine pronouns and images for God and comparisons of fathers and husbands with Jesus suggest male *role modeling*. In a world of family dysfunction, families were not the models for God. God and Jesus were the model for families. Biblical texts teach that men are to model their lives after God and Jesus rather than to see themselves as a god. How does God model male leadership?

GOD MAINTAINS RELATIONSHIP

First, *God is a God who maintains relationships.* I find that in domestic violence, the victim, usually the woman, is blamed for causing the marriage to fail. We generally attack the victim because we feel the burden falls on her. This is a misunderstanding of covenant. The burden falls on the husband. One biblical passage that illustrates the responsibility of the husband is Ephesians 5:21–33, which is built around this fundamental principle.

> Submit to one another out of fear/respect for Christ. (Eph 5:21)

Christian marriage is shared power. Both partners respect and submit to one another because they have a deep love for each other. Paul wrote this verse before he gave instructions to the wife and the husband. Before reading the rest of the text, men must acknowledge that a marriage is mutual submission and each man must work with his spouse for the health and development of their relationship and family.

> Wives, submit to your husbands as to the Lord. For the husband is the head of the wife as Christ is the head of the church, his body, of which

he is the Savior. Now as the church submits to Christ, so also wives
should submit to their husbands in everything. (Eph 5:22–24)

This was not written for husbands; therefore, it should not be quoted by
husbands to their wives. It is likely that this is a short section of instruction in
Ephesians because women in the first century were probably already submitting
to their husbands. However, in light of evidence concerning Roman women,
the plea only suggests that the wives continue to respect their husbands.[7]

Just as partners in Christian marriage are to submit to each other, ad-
ditionally the Spirit (1 Cor 14:32) is submissive to the prophets. God's Spirit
can be controlled and silenced by human beings. Does this indicate that God's
Spirit is less worthy than human beings? Submission says nothing about sta-
tus; it is only an act of giving, of support, and of encouragement. Women
and men submit to each other (Eph 5:21) in the ways God has shown them
through love, peace, compassion, and joy.

> Husbands, love your wives as Christ loved the church and gave himself
> up for her to make her holy, cleansing her by the washing with water
> through the word, and to present her to himself as a radiant church,
> without stain or wrinkle or any other blemish but holy and blameless.
> In this same way, husbands ought to love their wives as their own bod-
> ies. He who loves his wife loves himself. After all, no one ever hated his
> own body, but he feeds and cares for it, just as Christ does the church—
> for we are members of his body. For this reason a man will leave his
> father and mother and be united to his wife, and the two will become
> one flesh. This is a profound mystery—but I am talking about Christ
> and the church. However, each one of you also must love his wife as he
> loves himself, and the wife must respect her husband. (Eph 5:25–33)

This longer section of instruction was written to husbands. Why so long?
Is it possible that these men needed to change? Notice the model that Paul
used. Jesus is the model of compassion, love, concern, care, and gentleness.
When I describe a husband in these terms, in counseling, I never have a female state that she would not respect a man like this. Many times women state
that their husband thinks he's God. What "god" are they referring to? What
would happen if their husband acted like the real God?

Artemis was the goddess of fertility, war, and healing. She was the "head"
of Ephesus. Her cult following in this city was so strong that she was given
more recognition than the Roman cult of Caesar. When Jesus is called "head"

---

7. For more information on the New Roman Wives, their rebellion in the Roman culture, and
Paul's encouragement for the female Christian community, see Winter, *Roman Wives, Roman
Widows*, 17–30.

for the church at Ephesus, it is a direct parallel to Artemis. As the great mother, she nurtured and cared for the city. As the great head of the Christian community, Jesus nurtures and cares for the church. Jesus's example for husbands was not one of power but one like Artemis. He maintains relationship through love, support, and care. Husbands must practice love, compassion, honor, and mercy in their relationships with others, including their wives. This is the meaning of headship in Ephesians.

Maintaining a relationship means that men and husbands should act like Jesus. To oppress the poor and weak is a sign of unrighteousness. To defend and support the "weaker" one is a reflection of God's nature. A relationship with our wives should lift them up and bless them. If they feel worse by being in a relationship with us, it is our issue rather than theirs. Marriage should help both partners become better and feel better about themselves.

GOD DISPLAYS MERCY AND COMPASSION

Second, *God is a God who expects leaders to practice mercy and compassion.* There has been much discussion about male headship, but it comes from a lack of understanding concerning leadership. For the husband to be the head means that he provides leadership. What style of leadership? The husband must lead as God leads. In the Ephesians text quoted above, two issues of leadership are discussed.

The man leaves his parents in order to cleave to his wife (Gen 2:24; Eph 5:32–33). This cleaving is a covenant. His parents led him in covenant; now it is time for him to do the same with another woman. As one who cleaves to his wife, he has responsibilities to her as a husband. He is to provide her with support, mercy, love, and compassion. He is to help her develop so that she might be blameless before God. If her emotional, sexual, spiritual, or other needs are not being met, he should be listening to her to help her. With him in her life, she is to grow closer to God, not farther away.

Karen had been referred to me at her church. Her husband was in a local seminary, and she had left him because she claimed that he had been verbally and at times physically abusive to her. As she told me the story, she would, at times, question herself. The seminary seemed to support Thomas and communicated to Karen that she was wrong for leaving him.

"Maybe it is me. Maybe it is not as bad as I think," she said.

"Do you think the marriage is bad?" I asked.

"Yes, I guess so," she said. "But Thomas doesn't think it is that bad."

"What does Thomas say?" I asked.

"He thinks that I am causing the problems in the marriage. He says it is me. We have tried counseling but I seem to blow up and get mad. Then the counselor takes his side," she blurted out.

"Does the counselor take his side, or is that what Thomas tells you?" I questioned.

"Maybe a little of both," she sighed.

"Karen, I have a question for you. You have been separated from Thomas for three months. Do you feel better about yourself?"

"Yes," she immediately said.

"If you went back to him, how would you feel then?" I said.

"I would feel bad about who I am and would feel depressed," she responded.

"And does your relationship with Jesus make you feel better about who you are?"

"Yes, if I left Jesus I would feel worse," she said.

"That's interesting, Karen. If marriage is a reflection of Jesus's covenant with the church, then why do you feel better being away from Thomas? Shouldn't it be the other way around?" I asked.

"I see your point," Karen said as she nodded her head.

A healthy relationship should make us feel better about who we are.

> Husbands, in the same way be *considerate* as you live with your wives, and treat them with respect as the *weaker partner* as heirs with you of the gracious gift of life, *so that nothing will hinder your prayers.* (1 Pet 3:7)

The Apostle Peter tells the husbands to be *considerate* or gentle with their wives. The husband is the initiator/patron and the wife is the recipient/client in this covenant. When Peter calls her *the weaker partner*, he is not criticizing women; rather, he is making a statement to men. Just as God has a responsibility to humans, so the husband has a responsibility to his wife. Just as God ignores the pleas of those who oppress the poor, so *God will ignore the prayers of a husband who emotionally, physically, and spiritually starves or abuses his wife.*

> If someone shuts their ears to the cry of the poor they too will cry out and not be answered. (Prov 21:13)

> Husbands love your wives and do not be harsh with them. (Col 3:19)

Physically, verbally, and emotionally abusive men are in direct violation of what God has called them to be.

MALE PRIVILEGE AND CHRISTIAN THEOLOGY

Male privilege is not a right for men. Male privilege is a result of dysfunction and abuse. Male responsibilities are what spiritual men are called to fulfill. As husbands, we must initiate love and compassion in our marriages. Our role as "leaders" is to provide the emotional, spiritual, and physical needs of our wives and families. For centuries, wives have carried the weight of their marriages and children alone. They have wrestled with their children in church and then come home to be greeted by their husbands with, "What are you fixing for dinner?" They have covered scars, bruises, black eyes, and tears and have patiently suffered at the hands of men who felt it was their right to control them. Wives have given their hearts and lives to a Savior who, in their eyes, is a man. They have prayed to a God who is a Father even though many have had earthly fathers who were tyrants.

It is time that men become like the man Jesus proved to be. It is time that men become the spiritual ones that God has proven to be. It is time that men listen to God, who shows men how they ought to live. It is time that husbands love their wives as Jesus loves the church. It is time that men treat women as spiritual people, in the image of God. It is time that men grow up and provide for the spiritual, emotional, and psychological needs of those who trust them.

CHAPTER 6

ROADBLOCK 1: Till Death
Do Us Part?

IT IS EASY for someone who has not been abused to pass judgment on victims. Victims do not stay in their relationships because they enjoy being abused. They do not return to their husbands because they prefer the violence and humiliation. Victims are caught in a web of control, power, and violence, and for them to break free involves personal, emotional, and psychological risk. As mentioned in the first section, the dynamics of abuse and family dysfunction are hard to understand unless you have lived in that environment.

Imagine what it is like to leave your abusive partner. You wrestle the kids into the car and flee for your life. Your adrenaline is pumping, and you hope that you made the right choice. You are still shaking from the yelling and hitting, but you know you must stay calm for the kids. You call a shelter and there is no room. If you are lucky, you have a friend who will let you stay. If not, you may go to your parents' home, where you have seen your mother abused for years. You've tried to leave before, and your parents were mad at you for going back to him. In the past they have told you that the man you love is a bum; therefore, you decide to keep the details from your family. "We just had a fight," you say. Everyone tells you that it will blow over, and that you can go home tomorrow. It is crowded, and the kids want to go home; this is not a good visit to grandma's house. Maybe this was a bad idea.

If you had called the police, they may have taken him away in handcuffs. He was both cussing and threatening you, or he was crying and saying he loves you and it will never happen again. Your emotions of fear, confusion, and anger have been bottled up inside. The officer is a big man, pretty intimidating but nice, and he cannot get emotionally connected to you at this time. The domestic-violence advocate cannot come, because the city has cut out the program and left it on the shoulders of the already-overworked detectives. The officer tells you that since you live in Oregon, your husband will be prosecuted for this crime (if you live somewhere else, you may have to file charges yourself) and suggests you get a restraining order to keep him away.

The flashing lights from the police car have drawn the attention of the neighborhood, so you try to hide your face and smile as if it were just a little incident. You go inside the house where the children are screaming, crying, and wondering when Daddy will come home. Your oldest daughter is in the corner, and she tells you that if he sets foot in the house again, she is leaving. Your son is in another corner with a knife in his hand and says, "If he comes back I swear to God I'll kill him!" The other children are asking why you had the bad policeman come and take Daddy to jail. After a few hours, you manage to get the kids in bed and lay your head down. Maybe it will be better in the morning. Maybe you don't need to file the restraining order. Maybe he'll come home tomorrow, and we'll forget the whole thing happened.

If you are brave enough to get a restraining order at city hall, you will try to call in sick from work. You'll resurrect the emotionally drained children and drop them off at school or the sitter's house, saying, "I can't pay you now. Can I pay you later?" You will fight the traffic, and if you are in Portland, you'll try to find a parking place. If you can find one, the meter is expensive and only good for three hours. Now you will have to walk three blocks to City Hall. You will go through the metal detectors, climb the stairs, and find the small room with the ten-page restraining-order application. This application is complicated, and it will take at least an hour to complete. The advocate is very nice, but she is bilingual and in demand from others. She does a great job of helping you as well as the other five women in the room. The form is confusing. You need to know what is in your home, what guns he owns, and how many times he has hit and threatened you in the past few months. It's all running together in your mind, but you have to get the papers done by noon so that you can go before the judge at one o'clock. (When you think about seeing the judge at one o'clock, you think, *Great! The parking-meter fare will run out by then. I am going to have to come up with more money!*) The advocate is helpful and supportive but cannot tell you what to write on the restraining-order form.

Then you wait for a few hours. There is no place to get lunch, so you skip it. At 1:00, you go before the judge. "I hope the judge is not a man. I am afraid of men in power," you sigh. Your prayers are answered, and the female judge finally gets to you. "So many women are in here for restraining orders. Am I one among many today?" The judge is compassionate and kind and explains everything to you. It is nice not to be talked down to! She has the clerk stamp the restraining order, and you are asked to go downstairs to talk to the sheriff's deputies.

The sheriff's employees are nice, but they are behind, so they quickly read the rules to you. You don't want to be a bother, so you only ask one question, "When can I go home?" They inform you that the restraining order will be served tomorrow (unless this is a Friday). "If he answers the door, he will be served. If not, we keep trying until he is home. The order of protection takes affect only when we physically serve him the papers," they inform you. "You might want to stay with a friend until he is served." You think, *why did I ask such a dumb question? There are a million others I should have asked.* You stay with a friend but feel that you are an imposition. This time you tell your friend that you won't go back to him like you did last time. Your children are angry and emotional, and they wonder when Dad will be home, and ask you out of fear, not concern. Your friend is struggling to pay the bills and is strapped emotionally, so the next three days will be tense and confusing.

After three days at your friend's house, you go home to a house that your husband has trashed. Your favorite pictures have been broken, and he left a note over the old wedding picture, "Please forgive me!" The deputy who accompanied you suggests that you change the locks and notify the neighbors so you can be safe. ("That's great," you say. "Now everyone knows we can't keep our family together.") You go to church on that Sunday, hoping that God and the church will help you and the kids in this horrible time of your life. Will you hear an encouraging sermon about how God and the church take a stand to protect victims? Will you see children with their dads playing and laughing? Will anyone recognize you or notice the bruises? Or will you hear that divorce is bad, that all marriages have ups and downs, that forgiveness is a virtue, or that your church's evangelism team is targeting two-parent homes with children?

I met someone once who felt good about leaving her husband until she went to church.

I came to the shelter to visit Cecilia and see how she was doing. Two weeks earlier I had been involved in mediation between her counselors and the men who were counseling her husband (which I discussed earlier, in chapter 1). She had been strong in her refusal to return to Robert or give him conjugal visits. She shared with me that throughout her life and marriage some person always seemed to be there to invite her to church, to listen to her, or to encourage her to leave her abusive relationships.

"Do you believe that God sends people to help us?" I asked.

"Yes, I do. Do you think these men and women were from God?" she responded.

"It wouldn't surprise me," I said.

"But they tried to get me out of the house and away from family," she said.

"Were you being abused during these times?"

"Sometimes, but usually it was when bad things were happening to me," Cecilia replied.

"Do you think that God was trying to get you out and help you to be safe?" I probed.

"I am very confused," she said. "And I need your advice. Last Sunday I went to church, and the minister said that Satan is breaking up families. Satan is causing families to divorce. Maybe I should go back to my husband. It seems that Satan wants me to be away from my husband."

I opened a Bible to Matthew 10:34–36 and showed these verses to her.

Do not suppose that I have come to bring peace to the earth. I did not come to bring peace, but a sword. For I have come to turn a man against his father, a daughter against her mother, a daughter-in-law against her mother-in-law. One's enemies will be those of their own family.

"Do you think that Jesus will split up a family if one person is devoted to God and the other opposes God?" I asked.

"I see your point," she said. "I guess I was just feeling guilty because I had left my husband, and I saw so many church women sitting with theirs that Sunday morning. I guess the sermon also made me feel a little guilty."

This is all too common when we encourage abuse victims to attend church. They sit in the pews and see healthy families (or those that appear to be healthy) and feel guilty. They hear sermons critical of divorce and how Satan is causing the breakdown of the family. They hear how Jesus overcame evil by submission and endurance. They hear that marriage is not about happiness but commitment. They hear how we are victims of the wickedness of society, and that hope, prayer, and endurance will bring us victory. Of all the people in the congregation, they are probably listening most intently to what is being preached. They return home with feelings of guilt because they have taken a stand for themselves, their children, and the truth—only to find it unwelcome in our worship services. Our government has empowered our civil servants to confront evil, yet we tell them to endure evil. Enduring evil can cause victims to stay victims. The person caught in abuse seems to feel that she has no alternative and is not able to leave or get help. Because she feels that she have no alternatives, she faces barriers on the road to recovery. I call these barriers theological roadblocks on the road to healing.

Why Are There Roadblocks?

I believe that our cultural values and spiritual doctrines play a major role in preventing women from leaving their husbands. The cultural issues of male power also prevent men whom their intimate female partners have abused from going public. There is a sense of shame in asking help from outsiders and the authorities. The emphasis from awareness groups and the media has helped us to see the need to address domestic violence, but families in abuse still feel a sense of shame. No one wants others to believe that they cannot "manage their families."

Many families also see the government as an enemy rather than an ally. Yet *God has given our government this right to protect citizens because the community of faith has failed to do the job of protecting women and children from abuse and oppression.* Statistically, victims of abuse who want protection from an abuser seek help from family, friends, and the spiritual community rather than the police.[1] Victims seek help from those with whom they have a relationship. Many domestic-violence advocates, however, feel that churches and family members are some of the most ineffective at providing services for victims. We have failed to empower victims as our government agencies have done. Is it possible that the government agencies are God's tool to protect the oppressed, who cry out for justice? Is it possible that the effectiveness of these government agencies is a reflection of the church's inadequacies? Is it possible that the effective work of government agencies to empower victims is a judgment against the faith community? Has the faith community empowered abusers to continue to abuse?

How does the faith community become an enabler in the abuse cycle? We hold to spiritual doctrines that further victimize victims and that keep abusers abusing. We turn our heads to the cries of the oppressed. We confront victims rather than abusers, and call for submission rather than justice. We place the roadblocks of *marriage and divorce issues, parenting issues,* and *issues of victimization* in front of the victims and unknowingly prevent them from leaving abusive relationships. In the rest of this chapter, we will discuss the first of these issues: marriage and divorce.

Marriage and Divorce

Marriage and family teachings in our spiritual communities are filled with presuppositions, false allegations, and warped perceptions of what a healthy

---

1. In Australia 67 percent of ministers were sought out by domestic-violence and child-abuse victims from their congregations, and by strangers (Dixon, "Clergy as Carers," 126).

family is meant to be. Much of this stems from our lack of understanding of covenant and its responsibilities to marriage and family. I have heard ministers teach that victims are bound to a covenant even when the partner is unfaithful. I have heard churches tell victims that being divorced is a sin and more damaging to children than being in a dysfunctional relationship.

The Marriage Covenant

GOD AND THE COVENANT

God establishes covenant with the creation. The marriage relationship is similar to this covenant. The covenant is holy and calls for faithfulness from *both partners* and is a "contract" with stipulations and obligations. I have found that many ministers and Christians believe that God carries the burden in the covenant with humans and expects little in return. They believe that God's covenant is not conditional, and that God keeps the relationship with humans regardless of their actions. The biblical texts suggest that in covenant humans have a responsibility to honor and respect their God.

> As originally written, there was no distinction between "covenant" and "contract." There is only one word for both . . . and there is no reason to believe that this one word represented more than one type of agreement. This applies not only to the OT [Old Testament] use of the term "covenant" but also to its use in the NT [New Testament] and beyond into the Church Fathers. Throughout this period, the term "covenant" meant a contract that could be broken if either side reneged on their half of the agreement.[2]

Covenant has always been two-sided. God promises to be faithful to humanity and expects the same loyalty from the creation. Since marriage is a reflection of a covenant between God and humans and between Christ and the church, loyalty within the covenant should reflect shared faithfulness.

The covenant can be broken. God is faithful and loyal to the covenant and to the children (Deut 7:9–11; Titus 1:4). But humans, historically, have violated this holy relationship (Heb 8:7–13; Jer 11:8). When the covenant is broken or violated, the offended party has two options: to punish or to forgive. In the Bible, God displays both options in the covenant. God has punished the unfaithful and has forgiven them.

> Yahweh will call you back as if you were a wife deserted and spiritually distressed, a young wife, rejected, says your God. For a little while I *abandoned* you, but with compassion I will bring you back. In a surge of

2. Instone-Brewer, *Divorce and Remarriage in the Bible*, 17.

anger I turned my face from you, for a moment, but with faithfulness I will have compassion on you says *Yahweh* your redeemer. (Isa 54:6–7)

I gave faithless Israel her *certificate of divorce* and sent her away because of all her adulteries. (Jer 3:8)

This is what Yahweh says: "Where is your mother's *certificate of divorce* with which I sent her away? Which creditor did I sell you to? You were sold because of your sins; because of your transgressions your mother was divorced." (Isa 50:1)

The peoples of Israel and of Judah were taken captive by Assyrian and Babylonian kingdoms in the seventh and sixth centuries BC respectively. Through the years God's patience was tested as the people turned their backs on their Creator. The Babylonian and Assyrian captivities are strong examples of God's punishing those who break the covenant. Yahweh describes these events as an abandoning or divorce of the people. God refused to show compassion and to protect Israel and Judah when they had violated the covenant.

Therefore this is what Yahweh says, "I will bring on them a disaster they cannot escape. *Although they cry out to me I will not listen* . . . Do not pray for this people nor petition for them, *because I will not listen when they call to me* in the time of their distress." (Jer 11:12)

They greatly love to wander; they do not restrain their feet. So Yahweh does not accept them; and will now remember their wickedness and *punish them for their sins."* Then Yahweh said to me, "Do not pray for this people. Although they fast, *I will not listen to their cry,* though they offer burnt offerings and grain offerings, *I will not accept them.* Instead, *I will destroy them* with the sword, famine, and plagues." (Jer 14:9)

Why is God so harsh? God had been faithful to the nation of Israel; however, Israel had not been faithful in their covenant. The prophetic books illustrate that God confronted Israel concerning their disregard for the covenant. Yet the nation's leaders ignored God's pleas for respect, love, and loyalty. The Israelites were acting as a husband who ignores his wife, who abuses her, and who is sexually, emotionally, and psychologically unfaithful to her. They were acting as a wife who humiliates her husband and is unfaithful to him. The covenant relationship had become a dysfunctional relationship. God was dishonored and humiliated because people were unfaithful (Isa 52:5; Ezek 36:22). God's name was to be glorified and honored among other nations. God deserved to be respected as a God of love, mercy, and truth. *God's practice of divorce was an aggressive action to protect the sanctity and purity of covenant.* The covenant relationship became dysfunctional because of humans. God found fault with the people, not the covenant. Yahweh had to become *overfunctioning* to keep the covenant, while Israel continued to *underfunction* due to their sin and neglect. God could not tolerate this type of relationship and divorced Israel for the sake of the covenant. God punished them for the sake of honor. Divorce, likewise, is an aggressive action to maintain the honor of covenant relationship.

Marriage, as a covenant, is a contract with stipulations and obligations, and also requires loyalty from both individuals. By *loyalty* I am not referring only to sexual faithfulness but also to issues of respect and shared power. Marriage is a reflection of God's covenant and relationship to Israel (Jer 3:8; Ezek 16:1–10) and of Jesus's relationship to the church (Eph 5:25; Rev 21:2). When we fail to love, honor, and respect God, we violate the covenant. When one spouse fails to love, honor, and respect the other, that partner (usually not the victim) violates the covenant. Divorce is not the problem but how the spouse is treated, honored, and loved. The victim, as does God, has the option to call the other to repentance and challenge them to holiness.

GOD THE FAITHFUL?

Christians and ministers may question these concepts from the prophets and wonder how God could punish people and abandon them. There tends to be a strong reaction to any thought of God punishing even the wickedest of people and allowing them to perish. Our perspective on what it means to be God is sometimes a lose-lose situation. If God condemns my loved ones, God is unjust. If God forgives my enemies, God is a monster. If God punishes, God is abusive. If God does not act, God is nonexistent. It seems that our concept of covenant is tied into this perspective of God. God is to be faithful, so we believe, regardless of my actions. We believe that covenant cannot be a two-way street, because we are too weak for that. We believe that covenant is a one-sided relationship, where God *overfunctions* for those of us who *underfunction*.

Humans make mistakes. We are weak, and only God is perfect. We have the ability to resist the temptation to sin, and we are never tempted with more than we can resist (1 Cor 10:13)! Therefore, living in covenant is a marriage with God. God is full of mercy, grace, love, and patience, and helps us in our relationship. While we struggle in our walk with God, we receive grace and mercy to continue in that relationship. However, God does not turn a deaf ear to rebellion, unfaithfulness, and neglect. God promises to be faithful but also expects us to be faithful. In covenant there is always an understanding of shared responsibility.

> The Old Testament speaks of marriage as a "covenant" . . . which was
> the ancient Near Eastern term for any kind of binding agreement
> or contract. The correct phrase for a marriage agreement in the Old
> Testament is therefore a "marriage contract." Like any other contract,
> this contained an agreement and penalties for breaking the agreement.
> The penalty for breaking the marriage contract was divorce with loss
> of the dowry.[3]

The prophets tell us that God did reconcile with the Israelites. God eagerly desired to forgive them and brought them home from Babylon. The nation's repentance (Daniel 9; Jeremiah 29) and desire to be faithful to God renewed their covenant and brought the promise of hope and peace to those abandoned by God. This promise came, by the grace and mercy of Yahweh, as a new start. But God still expected them to continue in obedience and loyalty while in the covenant.

> If you will walk in my ways and keep my requirements, then you will
> govern my house and have charge of my courts, and I will give you a
> place among these standing here. (Zech 3:7)

The covenant requires faithfulness from *both* parties. The consequences of breaking the covenant rest on the offender. The offended party has the right to punish or forgive. When Israel broke the covenant with God, God many times forgave them. Yet God also chose to punish by divorcing the nation of Israel. God did this because the covenant had become dysfunctional. The nation of Israel was shamelessly violating the trust and loyalty that Yahweh had given to them.

The same is true in marriage. Both parties are expected to be faithful to the covenant. When dysfunction rules the marriage, the covenant and spouse are in danger of being dishonored or violated. The offended spouse has the option to confront the other individual and call the person to repentance. The dysfunctional spouse has the option to repent and work toward healing in the marriage or risks being cut off from the relationship.

DOESN'T GOD HATE DIVORCE?

Another theological objection to God's divorcing Israel is the verse often quoted from Malachi 2:16: "I hate divorce, says Yahweh the God of Israel."[4] Many, especially clergy and abusers, have used this text to tell victims that

---

3. Instone-Brewer, *Divorce and Remarriage in the Bible*, 19.

4. Other versions of the Hebrew suggest alternate English translations of this verse. Some versions read, "If you hate her, divorce her." For more information on the validity of this translation, one can consult Berlin et al., *Jewish Study Bible*, 1272.

God does not approve of divorce. While I believe that divorce can be traumatic to a family, I find that Yahweh practiced divorce in Israelite history (Isa 50:1; 54:6–7; Jer 3:8). These texts seem difficult to reconcile with the view that God opposes any divorce.

In the book of Malachi, the nation of Judah has returned from Babylonian/Persian captivity (538/535 BC). They have been challenged by Haggai and Zechariah to rebuild the temple of God (Hag 2:1–9; Zech 2:7–13). God reminds them that they can start over and become holy (Hag 2:19). As time passes, they begin to return to the ways of their former generations by neglecting the sacrifices and practicing idolatry (Mal 1:1–6). While God was the offended husband in the prophecy of Hosea, God becomes the offended wife in Malachi 2:11–16.[5] Israel has married a foreigner and has begun to practice injustice. The people of Israel again practice the same behavior that had caused the previous divorce. How is God to respond to this behavior?

First, God, as the offended spouse, *warns the people to stop violating the covenant.* They had left the wife of their youth (Yahweh) and married a foreign goddess (most likely Asherah). Second, *the book of Malachi may not be talking about marriages between people but about Judah's covenant with God.* The book is filled with references to their covenant with God and about how they are violating this relationship. The prophet is warning the nation because God hates divorce—however, God will practice it. Finally, *the text also suggests that God hates one who covers oneself with violence.* We should be more concerned about those who are violent in their relationships, because God is clearly condemning their actions.

> "I hate divorce," says Yahweh, God of Israel. "And I hate a man covering himself with violence as his garment . . ."

Malachi 2:16 does not suggest that God is angry with divorced people. The text is a warning to those who are unfaithful *and violent* in their relationships with Yahweh and *other humans.* The text is calling people back to God. It confronts those contributing to violence and dysfunction in the covenant and relationship. While God hates divorce, God practiced divorce. Divorce is not something that God is eager to initiate, but it is an option in order to keep the covenant holy and honorable. While God accused Israel of sexual promiscuity (idolatry), God equally condemned them for social injustice and

---

5. For texts that suggest God as mother, as wife, or as female, see Isa 42:14; 46:3; 66:9–13. John 4 suggests that God is spirit (which reminds us that gender is not a characteristic of God). In the biblical texts, female imagery is used of God as well as male imagery. See Smith, *Origins of Biblical Monotheism*, 90.

violence. Israel was divorced not only for idolatry but also for social injustice, violence, and oppression (Isa 1:21–23).

JESUS AND DIVORCE

Jesus also spoke on the issue of divorce. In Matthew 19 he says, "I tell you that anyone who divorces his wife, except for marital unfaithfulness, and marries another woman commits adultery." To some, this seems to be the only reason Jesus gives for divorce. There are a few considerations on this point. First, Jesus is speaking to Pharisees who are questioning him and trying to find a reason for divorce. That Pharisees were trying to find reasons for divorce is evident in the collection of rabbinical writings and traditions circulating around the time of Christ.[6] The rabbis had developed a complex method of validating divorce that in many ways victimized the women. In Luke 16:15–18, Jesus accuses them of trying to justify themselves, and he uses divorce as an example of this. Both Matthew and Luke suggest that Jewish men, especially Pharisees, sought reasons to divorce their wives and further victimize them. The Jewish practice of divorce had also become highly influenced by the Greco-Roman culture and the freedom it gave to men to divorce their wives. Jesus's discussion about divorce and remarriage was not designed to be a discussion of all forms of divorce but a *prohibition against men's victimizing their wives*, something that was common practice in the first century. According to Jesus, marriage was not an institution designed to victimize women.

The Apostle Paul further discusses issues of Christian marriage in 1 Corinthians 7. Paul suggests that marriage is important for men and women in order to share sexual intimacy and fulfill each other's sexual desires (1 Cor 7:1–6). Paul reminds married Christians that the Lord Jesus had commanded them not to divorce (1 Cor 7:10–11). This command prevented one spouse from either victimizing or neglecting the needs of the other.[7] According to Paul, marriage is still a covenant that required *both* husband and wife to work together for love, security, and faithfulness.

Concerning the issue of mixed marriages (a Christian married to a non-Christian), Paul advises that the Christian is not to seek a divorce if the unbelieving spouse is willing to stay in the relationship.

> To the rest I say, not the Lord, that if any brother has a wife who is an
> unbeliever, and she is willing to live with him, do not divorce her. And

---

6. The Mishnah is a collection of rabbinic writings from 200 BC to around AD 200. The so-called *Gittin* section is a large tract that gives suggestions concerning legal divorce and reasons one might divorce a spouse.

7. Instone-Brewer, *Divorce and Remarriage in the Bible*, 189–212.

> if a woman has a husband who is an unbeliever, and he is willing to live
> with her, do not divorce you husband. (1 Cor 7:12–13)

This teaching became a problem because Roman society was quite different from the Jewish and Christian communities in regard to morality. This
difference was especially marked concerning husbands and their treatment of
wives and children. Roman men were sometimes encouraged to be promiscu-
ous, and to be harsh with their families. Roman wives had also been given
many freedoms and could divorce their husbands and remarry. By the time
of Paul, Roman culture had so affected the family that divorce was common
even among Jews.[8] Yet the Christian was to be different and practice faithfulness in marriage.

Christians also had the right to expect to be treated fairly and honorably
even if they were married to a non-Christian. Paul believed that the Christian
spouse should still expect faithfulness, loyalty, and respect even from an
unbelieving" spouse. In 1 Corinthians 7:12–14, Paul suggests that keeping a
marriage together (meaning that spouses agree to live with each other) brings
a sense of holiness to the family.

> For the husband makes the unbelieving wife holy, and the wife makes
> the unbelieving husband holy, otherwise your children would be un-
> clean but now they are holy. (1 Cor 7:14)

Both Christian and non-Christian could work together to bring holiness, love,
and purity to their families. The Christian was encouraged to communicate
with a spouse in order to work through the relationship, which would be a
great witness for Jesus.

This would not have been possible in every marriage. In mixed marriages where the unbelieving spouse was not willing to honor Jesus and live
in a healthy relationship (as described in 1 Corinthians 7:1–9), the Christian
spouse was not bound to the marriage. Actually, Paul writes:

> But if the unbeliever wants to depart, let them go. The brother or sister
> is not bound in this, for God has called us to peace. How do you know,
> wife, if you can save your husband and how do you know, husband, if
> you can save your wife? (1 Cor 7:15–16)

While this seems harsh to many, Paul was not as concerned about the
state of marriage as much as he was about the health and peace of the family.
If the unbeliever brought abuse and sin to the family and neglected the wife,
Paul allowed for divorce.

8. This is also evident in Herod's encouragement for Herodias to marry him after she had
been coaxed into divorcing his brother Philip (Luke 3:19–20).

Paul also mentions that God has called all Christians to peace. A home with abuse, alcoholism, drug addiction, pornography, fighting, extramarital affairs, or hatred of another's religious convictions is not a home of peace. Paul's concern is for the Christian who would be subjected to sin through the other spouse. Paul is challenging the Christian to take a stand and to call the family to holiness. The Christian should set the standard behavior for the family. Christians are not expected to let their abusive spouses rule the home and bring violence to the children. The children need to be holy and live in a house of peace. The Christian has every right to demand and expect peace and respect in the home. The Christian has the right to confront an abusive, alcoholic, drug-addicted, or sex-addicted spouse and say, "As long as we are married, this behavior will not continue." Many times the underfunctioning spouse agrees and receives help. This can bring peace to the family. At other times, the spouse manipulates or refuses to get help. Paul says, "Let them go."

I understand that this is difficult for many to accept, but Paul's position is grounded in a theology that wishes to help others become more like God. I have known wives who have confronted their husbands and have seen peace restored. I know of husbands who have addressed sin in their marriages and have reunited with their wives. I do not believe Paul was pushing for divorce; he was pushing for healthy families. For Paul, as for God, divorce was an aggressive action that protects the sanctity of the covenant as well as the home. As God confronted the men in Malachi to return to their covenant, so wives have the right to call their abusive husbands back to the covenant.

The Jewish faith community has also been a strong advocate for peace in the home (*shalōm bayit*). For this community, domestic abuse violates the peace and safety in the home, an issue that the Apostle Paul was obviously concerned about. Rabbis have suggested to me that the evangelical church's strong stance against divorce can become a stumbling block for victims and their children undergoing abuse. It seems that their criticism is fair since we have historically encouraged women to stay in abusive relationships even at the risk of peace in the home. Paul, however, suggests that a safe home is preferred over a dysfunctional or abusive marriage.

A New Context for Marriage

Traditionally we evangelical Christians have viewed the marriage covenant as beginning at creation when male and female were joined in the Garden of Eden.

There was no helper found to compliment Adam. So God caused Adam to fall into a deep sleep and took a bone from his side/rib and closed the flesh from where it was taken. God built the rib, which he had taken from the man, into a woman and brought her to the man. The man said, "This is now bone of my bones and flesh of my flesh. This one is to be called woman/wife because she was taken from man/husband." So a man leaves his father and mother and cleaves to his wife so that they may become one flesh. The two were naked and were not ashamed. (Gen 2:20b–25)

Male and female "complement" each other. Creation of males and females to complement each other is a divine act. Since God has made them one (Mal 2:15), they should cleave together. As Jesus stated, "They are no longer two but one flesh" (Matt 19:6). Marriage is not just a uniting of two people; it is a partnership that depends on two people working together. It is a mutual relationship. Jesus warns not only outsiders trying to divide a couple but also those in marriages who refuse to treat their spouse as a partner.

Since marriage is a reflection of the covenant, the question that should be addressed is, how does God want marriages to reflect the covenant?

As was discussed earlier, God's covenant with Israel allows for blessings or punishments. When Genesis 2 becomes the core biblical text on marriage, then the option of divorce is seen as splitting or dividing the one flesh. While divorce truly does divide the one flesh, focusing exclusively on this truth causes Christians to see divorce as the main problem in abusive marriages. This is how marriage and divorce have traditionally been approached. Marriage is the goal, and divorce signals the end of the relationship.

Figure 7: Traditional View of Marriage and Divorce

According to this view, the main problem for a marriage to avoid is divorce. As long as a couple does not divorce, they assume that they are doing God's will. The recent rise in divorce among American married couples has caused the church to react by focusing on keeping marriages together. While addressing the divorce issue is a great need among our churches, the problem in failing marriages is not divorce. Divorce is only a symptom of a bigger problem. Too many couples feel that they are reflecting God's covenant by just "staying together." They seem unconcerned about the fighting, dysfunction, and sin that may be lord of their marriage. In fact, they practice tolerance because they believe that God practices tolerance with us in the covenant.

This view is damaging to those who have left dysfunctional marriages and have divorced their spouses. Once individuals are divorced, they enter a spiritual no-man's-land where they struggle with guilt, and wonder if they could have done something differently to keep their marriage together. Divorce is seen as the problem and is blamed for the breakup of the family. When couples or individuals who are cohabiting come for counseling, I ask them why they do not get married. None of them tell me that they are afraid of divorce. They tell me that they are afraid of marriage. They do not describe marriage as a healthy, loving partnership. They point out that they see marriage as a relationship of fighting, arguing, celibacy, unfaithfulness, and abuse that cannot be broken. They see that marriage has an intended permanence to it, but as a form of slavery. Their mother and father could not leave each other, so their parents put up with dysfunction. The children, who come to see me, have learned that this is marriage.

This suggests to me that we should have a different view of marriage and divorce. We should address marriage and dysfunction according to figure 8.

Marriage ⸺→ Divorce

Figure 8: A New View of Marriage and Dysfunction

This view of marriage, dysfunction, and divorce suggests that the main problem for marriages to avoid is not divorce—it is dysfunction. Dysfunction exists when a marriage is not healthy. Dysfunction exists when there is not *mutual* submission, shared power, or mutual respect. Dysfunction exists when the couple does not communicate, does not resolve conflict in a healthy manner, or shares little intimacy, if any. Dysfunction exists when the covenant is broken or is in danger of being broken due to the actions of one or both spouses. Dysfunction exists when one or both spouses practice behavior that is contrary to God's will. Is every marriage dysfunctional? No. Can there be dysfunction in an otherwise healthy marriage? Yes. My point is that healthy marriages seek to address dysfunction while dysfunctional marriages try to "hang on to" or refuse to deal with the sin that exists between the couple.

Dysfunction can lead to divorce. It must be addressed in marriages, or the marriage may dissolve. If dysfunction does not end, the marriage may not be the type of marriage God has called the couple to have. Just as God called the people of Israel to repent of its dysfunctional relationship in the covenant, so a couple should be willing to repent of anything sinful or damaging in their marriage. In the case of abuse, the abuser must repent, and the victim should feel empowered to expect to be treated with love, respect, and mercy.

The church can be effective at addressing dysfunction in married couples by encouraging this model rather than bashing divorce. In the last thirty years, our attempts to address divorce have not been effective, and we have seen an increase in divorce among Christians. Divorce-care ministries have also increased, and these ministries have been at the forefront of fighting the feelings of shame and guilt, and of trying to encourage members to see that divorce is not the end of their lives. Yet divorce continues to happen even though the faith community has condemned it. I have noticed that we Christians blame society for divorce, and we point out the influence of society on our marriages. Yet we have not addressed or identified the real problem. Dysfunction is the problem. Dysfunction continues in marriages; but Christians believe they are doing the will of God as long as the couple stays together. We have preached about a faithful God and Savior who will do anything to keep the marriage together, yet we have ignored texts that suggest that God divorced those abusing the covenant. We have created confusion, caused resentment or even worse, and become dysfunctional in our own understanding of covenant and marriage.

As the church, our role, instead, should be to encourage healthy marriages. Our churches should focus on addressing dysfunctional behavior in marriages by calling for marriages to reflect God's covenant. God's covenant is a model for marriages, and God's covenant expects the practice of mutual love, mercy, and justice within that covenant. We have a great opportunity to strengthen marriage and indirectly cause a decrease in divorce. We have the opportunity to call people to repentance before they go to the lawyer. Yet we also have the opportunity to call individual spouses to take a stand and be empowered to leave spouses who refuse to reflect the glory and love of God. These spouses can then grow stronger in their faith rather than become overcome with guilt.

ABUSE AND THE MARRIAGE COVENANT

Abuse is a violation of a covenant between two individuals. A man who abuses his wife does not do so out of respect and love for her. He is attempting to control her. A man who verbally humiliates and degrades his wife is not trying to promote peace in the home; he is destroying the bond of peace that once existed. *Since the abuser is violating the marriage covenant, the abuser must be confronted, not the victim.* Too often the community of faith attempts to force the victim to keep the marriage together. Covenant is a shared responsibility, and when it becomes one-sided, the underfunctioning partner violates it. Victims have been humiliated and shamed into returning to their abusive spouses. Faith communities give victims false hope that they can outserve the evil in their partner. This is not theologically sound and is dangerous to victims. Holiness should be restored to the marriage covenant by addressing the abuse within the relationship. Holiness comes by confronting sin rather than ignoring it.

Abusers Need to Be Confronted

First, *the abuser must be confronted* concerning the sin of abuse and manipulation. An abuser's commitment to the relationship and to God is reflected in how he treats his spouse. I do not suggest that victims do this but those called by God as leaders should confront abusers. Questions such as, "How does beating your wife glorify God?" or, "How does God expect you to treat your spouse?" are important to address with an abuser. I have found that abusive men tend to point out why their wives cannot leave them, but they fail to admit that they are the cause of the marriage problems. In Malachi 2:16, God confronts the dysfunctional partner in covenant, not the victim. The abuser must be confronted for their behavior because they are the ones violating the covenant, not the victim.

Jesus's statements concerning marriage and divorce can also apply to abusers. Jesus's definition of adultery as looking at women and lusting was a challenge to men to stop treating women as objects (Matt 5:27–30). Jesus's prohibition against divorce for any reason except sexual immorality (adultery) is another statement about husbands' victimizing their wives (Matt 5:31–32; 19:1–9). Jesus was telling the Pharisees that they needed to stop looking for ways to find fault with their wives, and to be sexually faithful to them. Jesus clearly taught that marriage is a relationship where men are not to victimize their wives. The Apostle Peter carries this thought by reminding men that God will not hear their prayers if they are harsh with their wives (1 Pet 3:7).

From a theological point of view, abusers violate many teachings of the Bible and the sanctity of the covenant if they are verbally, physically, sexually, or emotionally abusive and neglectful to their spouses. Marriage is not a relationship of enslavement, manipulation, control, or abuse. It is a relationship of empowerment, respect, support, grace, mercy, and shared power. It is a relationship similar to that of God and Israel and of Jesus and the church. Abusers, rather than victims, need to be charged with violating the covenant. Abusers need to know that God, their spouses and families, the faith community, and our society oppose their behavior and will call them to repent. Victims need this support and should understand that leaving their abusers, seeking help and healing, and confronting this sin should be done, because the marriage covenant needs to be made holy.

When confronting abusers, one must remember that they can be manipulative and coercive. They may use minimization and denial concerning the sin of abuse. Abuse is not about anger; it is about control. They are not monsters; they are simply individuals who, like many of us, are afraid to get caught. They will resort to blaming the victims, police, their families, work and stress, you, or their background for their behavior. They need to be reminded that repentance is not about them; it is about validating victims and making things right with God.

Abuse is a sin; no one deserves to be physically or emotionally humiliated. Our role in the faith community is to call abusers to repentance and to turn them toward God. This means that we do not judge, but that we confront them and give them the chance to repent. We have a legal system and many counselors who can make the decisions about the guilt or innocence of the abuser according to the law.

Victims Need Safety

Second, *victims need to know that leaving their abuser is well within their rights as a child of God*. God does not oppose their move to safety and healing. God confronts the sin of abuse. The victim does not need to feel guilty or ashamed for leaving and protecting themselves and their family. Marriage is not bondage, and the victim is not bound to stay in a relationship with one who practices evil rather than good. Victims should be encouraged to grow, and to develop a sense of self-worth in Christ as children of God.

My students in Albania were amazed to hear that an advocate from their local abuse shelter indicated that the women should submit to their abusive husbands with the hope of overcoming this abuse. My students had spent a week in my Gospel of Luke class and were well aware that confronting the abuser is a role for the church They were surprised that their shelters encouraged women to return to their husbands and try to help their husbands stop being abusive by supporting them. I had to point out that at that time many countries wouldn't arrest an abuser due to cultural issues. One day that will change. Their role as young Christians is not to judge but to speak out and to call their society and government to address this issue and to provide for the safety of women and children. Christians should also hold men accountable for their actions. Until societies change, we all need to let victims know that they have rights.

One right victims have is *to be safe*. Since the marriage covenant is to provide them love, support, and respect, they have the right to be in an environment where these needs are met. If their marriage does not reflect the fruits of the Spirit (Gal 5:22–26), then they have the right to find safety. Victims have the right to call the police, to bring in outside intervention, to seek help from a shelter or family member, or to press charges against their abusive partner. Sometimes outside intervention is necessary to provide balance and bring back shared power to an individual's life. A family caught in abuse has one person, the abuser, in control. Shared power includes both partners' working together to empower each other to develop. The victim needs to be empowered; there may need to be an equalization of power in their lives. This can only happen by breaking the abuse and dependency cycles and keeping the victim and family safe. Every woman has the right to sleep at night knowing that she is safe.

Another right is the victim's *right to choose*. Many women who leave their abusive husbands are immediately pushed by faith communities to forgive. *Forgiveness is a choice.*

- God chose to enter a covenant with humans.
- God chose to ignore the sins of a few people.
- God chose to punish the Israelites.
- God chose to forgive and bring them back to Jerusalem.
- God chose to send Jesus. Jesus chose to lay down his life.
- Jesus chose to forgive.

We should never assume that God's forgiveness is forced. God can do whatever God wants (that's the advantage of being God). *Yet God overwhelmingly chooses to forgive.* "But it is in God's nature to forgive," I am told. This is true; but the Bible shows us many times when God does not forgive. When we pray, we should thank God for choosing to forgive us and to love us. We should never assume that God will be forced into a decision, and we should never assume we could manipulate God into forgiving.

Forgiveness is also a process. The people of Judah remained in Babylonian captivity for seventy years. During this time they had the opportunity to reflect on their sin. The seventy-year process helped the people to repent and prepare for forgiveness and their return to Jerusalem.

Victims have the right to choose. They can choose to be angry and hurt. They can choose to prosecute and punish the abuser. When they first leave the abuser, they are hurting and full of fear and anger. With time they may choose to forgive, but it must be their choice. Forgiveness is a healing process. Forgiveness is a willing decision to *let go* of the pain and past sins of another. Forgiveness, however, is not the same as "reunion." David Livingston makes a distinction between forgiveness, reconciliation, and reunion.[9]

> When one examines intimate violence as it actually presents itself, one finds that reunion of the violated and the violator is not always an appropriate response. The desire for reunion . . . is partly the consequence of a mythic view of reconciliation as reunion. This ideal of reunion has also been placed on the relationship of intimate partners and has become a model, at times even a "Christian expectation," that after violence one "should" try to reunite with one's abuser. As the church (bride) and Christ (bridegroom) have been able to reunite, so the survivor (bride) and the perpetrator (bridegroom) should also be able to reunite. This view does not take seriously the dynamics of intimate violence and does not take into account the physical and psychological scarring that has occurred. Reconciliation should not be confused with nor conflated into reunion.[10]
>
> Reunion should never be the assumed solution, especially by a church, which often errs on the side of "saving marriages." Instead, reunion of the victim and the violator should be considered only after all precautions for the safety of the survivor are first met.[11]

Forgiveness, reconciliation, and reunion all suggest different levels of relationship. Forgiveness is the first step and has some preconditions.

Confrontation is an important first step to forgiveness.

> If your brother sins against you, go and explain this to him between you and he alone. If he listens, you have gained your brother. If not, take one or two others with you so that by the mouth of two or three

9. Livingston, *Healing Violent Men*, 81–82.

10. Ibid.

11. Ibid., 23.

witnesses this is confirmed. If he doesn't listen to them, then tell the church, and if he doesn't listen to the church, treat him as a Gentile or tax collector. (Matt 18:15–17)

In this lesson, Jesus suggests that relationships can be repaired or strengthened through confronting the sinner. Jesus did not offer a new teaching here, however. The prophets and prophetic books of the Old Testament are examples of this confrontation. God sent prophets to confront Israel so that the process of forgiveness could begin. In the same way today, the one who has offended another must be made aware of the sin. Society and the faith community must also confront abusers so that they understand that their behavior is unacceptable.

Indeed Jesus calls us in the church to confront this brother or sister in order to help him or her to see sin. Especially when they are supported by the faith community, batterer-intervention groups better provide this accountability to abusers, as opposed to individual counseling. That is, batterer-intervention groups offer a support network and the opportunity for recovering men to form relationships with other men who confront abusive behavior.

Such confrontation is essential because some victims may never heal until they are able to confront their abusers with their sin. This is scary for victims. It takes time for them to feel adequately empowered to go to the one who has offended them. Individuals whose abuser has died may need to go to the cemetery to confront the abuser at the tombstone. There can be a liberating quality to speaking out about one's pain and telling the abuser, or the representation of the abuser, how they feel.

Victims must not be forced to forgive. They must choose to forgive. Nevertheless, the parable of the unmerciful servant (Matt 18:21–35) has been used to coerce victims to forgive

"I canceled all your debt because you begged me and you should have had mercy on your fellow slave like I had on you." The king was angry and turned him over to the jailers to be tortured until he should pay all he owed" . . . This is how my heavenly Father will treat each of you unless you forgive your brother from your heart." (Matt 18:32–35)

In this parable, a king forgives an outstanding debt that his slave owes. The slave had begged for forgiveness and is freed from the debt. The slave then finds another slave who owes him much less than he had owed the king. The second slave also begs for forgiveness, but the first slave throws him into prison. The unmerciful servant is a man who punishes even after his friend repents. The point of the parable is that God will punish (and hand over to the torturers) those who refuse to forgive. This suggests that victims can work toward forgiveness. In this parable, forgiveness comes from the greater one to the lesser one. Those who are oppressed are not addressed in this story. Victims should not be forced to forgive but should be encouraged to choose to forgive. However, sinners must first be confronted with their sin and called to repentance.

Repentance is the next step to forgiveness. Repentance is behavior modification. In the Old Testament, when the nations heard the message of the prophets and repented, forgiveness followed close behind. Repentance is the point at which the victim is validated and hears something like the following from the victimizer: "I am the sinner, not you." "I chose to do evil, not you." When God warned Israel of coming judgment, they were called to repentance. When Israel failed to repent, God did not forgive; God punished. Too often, victims are told to forgive someone who is not repentant. Forgiveness can come without repentance, but reconciliation demands it.[12] Victims struggle with anger and fear, not because they are weak, but because they have not been validated. "My point so far has been to suggest that it is not unreasonable to make forgiveness contingent on sincere repentance. Such repentance at the very least opens the door to forgiveness and often to reconciliation."[13]

Batterer-intervention programs and victims' services constantly seek ways to validate victims and to call abusers to repentance. By providing financial support, avoiding harassment of the victim, attending counseling, and sometimes serving jail time abusers attempt to validate the victim. Retribution and compensation suggest that an abuser has taken responsibility for sins and will provide what had been withheld from their spouses and children.[14] Churches must also encourage abusers to show their repentance and provide support for their families (2 Cor 7:8–12).

> Reconciliation, in situations of intimate violence, invites the perpetrator, the survivor, and the community to greater and fuller life through the healing of wounded relationships. The violator is welcomed into the community after he has been through the process of contrition, confession, and satisfaction. The victim/survivor is welcomed into a supportive community and is not told that she must reunite with her ex-partner but, rather, is invited to join a community of compassion,

12. Kelman, "Reconciliation as Identity Change," 119.

13. Murphy, *Getting Even*, 36.

14. While Murphy suggests that retribution seeks to impose suffering on the abuser or criminal, I tend to share Livingston's view over Murphy's. Livingston's view of retribution relates to calling the abusive husband to responsibility for his family and to making sure that they are provided for. Schimmel suggests that vengeance and justice can be administered by neutral institutions, such as the legal system (Schimmel, *Wounds Not Healed by Time*, 22–25).

> advocacy, and protection . . . reconciliation, if it is to address the viola-
> tion within the interhuman sphere, must also address the anger and
> resentment of the survivor of violence. To heal this resentment does
> not involve forgetting the violation, but creating the conditions for the
> survivor's being able to wish the well-being of the penitent batterer.[15]

Repentance makes it easier for a victim to forgive, and that is one focus of our ministry at Agape Church of Christ. If an abuser chooses not to repent, a victim can choose either to be angry for the rest of her life or to forgive.

Finally, the victim can *choose to forgive*. Forgiveness simply means to let go, and reconciliation means the reestablishment of the spiritual relationship of brother and sister in Christ. A relationship of Christian fraternity is not the same relationship as a marriage relationship. If in one case, a victim is validated, she can let go of the anger and pain caused by another. In another case, the victim is not validated but is exhausted from the hatred and anger with which she has been living. At that point, she can choose to let go of her anger and move forward. In both cases, the victims make a choice to forgive. Forgiveness is also a process that takes time and healing. Those who violate the covenant of marriage cannot force the offended spouse to forgive. Neither can others force victims and survivors to forgive.

Can people choose to forgive? It is possible, but it must be seen as a process. For all members involved in domestic violence, forgiveness will be part of their spiritual development. Victims should never be forced to forgive, but they can be encouraged to develop forgiveness. At the core of who we are as a faith community is forgiveness.

> For if you forgive people when they sin against you, your heavenly fa-
> ther will also forgive you. But if you do not forgive people's sins, your
> father will not forgive yours. (Matt 6:14–15)

> Father, forgive them because they do not know what they are doing.
> (Luke 23:34)

> Lord, do not hold this sin against them . . . (Acts 7:60)

Through forgiveness, victims, children, and families let go of their anger and draw closer together. Through forgiveness, victims choose not to be like the abuser who is full of fear, anger, confusion, and low self-esteem. Victims and families can face the future with hope and can choose not to let the abuser determine their happiness and spiritual choices. Through forgiveness, victims stop blaming themselves for the past and realize that their choice to

---

15. Livingston, *Healing Violent Men*, 82.

be safe and to protect themselves and their children was made through hope. Through forgiveness, victims realize that God is a loving God who empowers them to be compassionate and merciful with themselves and others.

Few abusive marriages have been salvaged. Hope is held out for couples who have reunited after intervention and extensive abuse counseling. Yet this process takes time and healing. What is important is that we in the church protect victims and empower them to grow, to heal, to develop spiritually, and to follow the journey to forgiveness. Abusers should be called to accountability and follow the journey to repentance. If reunion is not possible, there can always be hope of reconciliation and of a relationship in which each spouse becomes a parental role model for the children: one parent models courage through confrontation, and the other models courage through repentance.

> What lies at the core of reconciliation is nothing less than the enchanting and overwhelming notion that even when a human has become so distorted and disfigured by egoism, rage, despair, and fear, that person will be embraced by the Christian community. The Christian community has within its treasure trove of symbols a call for reconciliation. We are called as Christians not to demonize those who act in evil ways but rather to call them to accountability and to love them. This required that we ferret out the true insights in this message of hope.[16]

16. Ibid., 65.

CHAPTER 7

ROADBLOCK 2: Keep It Together
for the Children?

> We believe therefore that the psychological distress observed in children exposed to domestic violence results not only from their witnessing of periodic acts of violence but also from exposure to a batterer, and to his parenting style, in everyday life; in fact, we believe that the phrase "children exposed to batterers" is often more accurate than the current phrase "children exposed to domestic violence." For closely related reasons, we find that a batterer's parenting cannot be assessed separately from his entire pattern of abusive behaviors, all of which have implications for his children.[1]

THIS QUOTATION FROM two well-respected batterer-intervention specialists comes as a result of growing concern over the presence of children in violent homes. Research continues to suggest that abusive parents have a detrimental effect on children. Witnessing acts of domestic violence, learning the process of power and control, and receiving emotional and physical abuse meant for their mothers damages children every day. Three million children are exposed to acts of domestic violence each year.[2] Over one-third of children in one study reported seeing violence used by fathers against mothers when a parent reported that no violence occurred. More than 50 percent of female victims of intimate violence live in households with children under the age of twelve. Children are killed in one-fifth of domestic-violence homicides or attempted homicides each year.[3] Children in abusive homes are at great risk for emotional and physical abuse. When their mother leaves their father, they are at even greater risk.

---

1. Bancroft and Silverman. *The Batterer as Parent,* 2
2. Ibid., 1.
3. Ibid.

I had taken the three boys to see their dad. This was my first real experience with domestic violence and divorce. I had recently finished college and was working at McDonalds while I figured out what I wanted to do with my life. I was a new Christian and was helping a small church in my hometown. One of my co-workers, Karen, and her husband, Joseph, had been coming to church and had given their lives back to God. After a few months, he started drinking again and was emotionally abusive to his wife and three sons. He constantly threatened to kill himself and would hold a gun to his head and scream, "Daddy's going to kill himself!" He had attempted suicide regularly since he was sixteen, and this thirty-two year-old man lived his life drinking, changing jobs, and terrorizing his family.

Karen had had enough and finally left Joseph. The small church of mostly older people couldn't understand why she would leave her husband. Those of us at work tried to help her and the kids. We took turns, because the church would not help. I would take the boys one night a week while she worked. I also would take the kids to see Dad every other weekend. As long as I was there, it was considered a supervised visit.

One afternoon I took them to see Joseph. I was playing with the two older boys (eight and six years old) and failed to see Joseph take the five-year-old into the house. Even when I realized that Joseph had the boy in the house, I stayed outside with the older boys because I didn't think anything would happen. Thirty minutes later Joseph yelled, "Ron, come here!"

I went inside and saw the youngest boy crying.

"He don't want to go," Joseph said. All the boys started crying and began saying that they didn't want to go. Joseph was crying and wailing, which made the boys cry louder.

"Boys, I'm sorry, but the law says we have to go. We can see Dad again, but Mom's waiting for you," I said.

The boys stopped crying and went to the car. I could tell Joseph was mad at me. I told him that I didn't have to bring the boys by, and that I was doing him a favor. "Next time don't play with their heads, or I'll stop bringing them by," I said. As we drove away, the boys quickly forgot about their sorrow and began to talk about seeing their mother.

Joseph was an emotionally abusive man. He continued to manipulate the children against their mother every opportunity he had. What I realized that day and many other days since then was that children can be abused even more when their mother leaves home. Visitation rights, weekends with an abusive dad, and phone calls from treatment centers or prisons are not always in the best interest of the children.

Children are affected in normal activities, fear, sleep problems, explosive outbursts, poor interaction socially, poor conflict resolution skills, and other problems . . . Research has shown that witnessing adult physical aggression is more disturbing to children than observing other types of adult conflict . . . Children as young as one year begin to regress into states later diagnosed as "mental retardation" when they were exposed to parental hostilities that never went beyond the verbal abuse level. It is important to note for the question of contact with the abuser that the symptoms of retardation quickly disappeared after the parents separated.[4]

The sources of emotional and behavioral difficulty for children of battered women are many, with the actual seeing or hearing of acts of violence being only the beginning. The presence in the home of a batterer, usually in the role of parent or stepparent, has a wide range of implications for family functioning. Batterers tend to be authoritarian yet neglectful parents, with far higher rates than nonbatterers of physically and sexually abusing children. Battering changes the nature of children's crucial relationships with their mother, through mechanisms that include undermining her authority and interfering with her ability to provide care. Batterers often engage in efforts to create divisions within the family and can be highly manipulative.[5]

The evidence seems clear. Children exposed to abuse and abusers are affected emotionally and physically. Lundy Bancroft and Jay Silverman suggest that children of batterers also suffer from traumatic bonding.[6] When their mother leaves her abuser, she usually does not have to visit with him. She takes out a restraining order, and he can have no contact with her—but this does not always include the children. Children then may be subjected to the same manipulative, authoritarian, and controlling father that their mother can now avoid. Children can learn from an abuser the following beliefs:

- Victims are to blame for the abuse.

- Violence is justified to impose one's will or resolve conflicts.

- Boys and men control, women and girls should submit.

- Abusers do not face consequences for actions.

- Women are weak, incompetent, stupid, or violent.

- Anger, rather than control and manipulation, caused the violence and is an excuse for this behavior.

4. Straton, "What Is Fair for Children of Abusive Men?" 5.
5. Bancroft and Silverman, *The Batterer as Parent*, 2.
6. Ibid., 37–41.

Children learn unhealthy behaviors from batterers. While some children are resilient enough to be unaffected by abusive behavior, the majority are emotionally scarred by their abusive fathers. We have blamed children's behavior problems on the trauma of divorce rather than on the modeling of dysfunctional behavior. Women in abusive relationships should be willing to leave their spouses, and the church should see this as a way to protect their families. In 1 Corinthians 7:16, Paul allows an unbelieving spouse to leave a marital relationship if the unbeliever does not want to stay in the marriage and support the Christian spouse so that there could be peace in the home: "Otherwise your children would be unclean, but as it is they are holy" (1 Cor 7:16).

Keeping it together for the sake of the kids can be more destructive than leaving for the sake of the kids.

Parenting Roadblocks

Many times, victims choose not to leave their abusive spouses because they feel they would be responsible for breaking up the family. Yet victims are not the ones damaging their children. Abuse is contrary to God's plan for the family as well as contrary to the Holy Spirit (Rom 12:9–15; Gal 5:20–26). The family is to be a place of peace, wholeness, and empowerment. Victims, especially mothers, need to know that they have the right to protect not only themselves but also their children. Rather than "keeping the family together," families in abuse need to be encouraged to work for peace in the home. Victims should be allowed to keep their children away from violence, manipulation, and controlling behavior.

Divorce is certainly a traumatic event for children. The breakup of the home, the visitations, the transferring from home to home on weekends and during the summer all affect the emotional stability of children. Research is clear on this issue. Fighting; arguing; confrontation among spouses, ex-spouses, and family; and using children as informants are some of the emotional tactics of couples experiencing divorce that are traumatic to children. The effects of divorce or the attitudes surrounding abuse make divorce even more traumatic.[7]

> Children are far better off—as a number of studies demonstrate—living in peace with their mother than being exposed to a man who abuses her. In fact, the studies indicate that children are better off living with a single parent than being around parents who fight frequently even *without* abuse . . . The research that purports to show how damaging

7. See Miller's quotations in chapter 1 of this volume, notes 13 and 14.

single mothering is to children has failed to control for income and for prior exposure to abuse, so that the difficulties observed are actually the effects of poverty and of the fact that many children witnessed abuse while their parents were together—and that is why the mother is now single.

It is worth noting that we never seem to hear reports claiming that children are damaged when they are raised by single *fathers.* The reality is that single parenting is difficult, exhausting, sometimes isolating work, but both women and men can do it well, and the world is full of well-adjusted, successful people who grew up with one primary parent, male or female. What matters above all is to live in a home where there is safety, love, and kindness—and adequate economic resources.[8]

We in the church attempt to call spouses to be Christian or moral in divorce by removing conflict from the presence of the children and by agreeing not to place the children in the midst of their battle. While this is difficult, it is possible, and I find that when a sense of peace is established between ex-spouses, reconciliation is more likely.

Children can develop normally in a single-parent home, but parenting will be difficult. In dysfunctional families (those with alcoholism, drug abuse, pornography, or domestic violence), the continued exposure to these behaviors is more damaging to children than removing them from the home. While our government understands that children should not be exposed to these behaviors, our churches seem to be unaware of the damage that can be caused in the home. I have found that many ministers have preached on the "evils of divorce" but have never been willing to discuss how children in dysfunctional families are at risk. Divorce may be traumatic for children, but domestic violence, alcoholism, drug abuse, and other dysfunctional behaviors can damage them physically, emotionally, and spiritually. A clear examination of the evidence should lead us to the conclusion that a peaceful and holy home is preferable to one steeped in sin and dysfunction. Should churches support divorce? The question should be, how can churches address dysfunction in the home?

Victims Need to Be Empowered

Victims need to be *empowered to leave their abusive spouses,* since this is one way to provide peace and safety for all those in the home. One reason victims must leave with their children is that *exposure to an abuser affects the children's emotional and physical development.* As was mentioned in chapter 2, children

8. Bancroft, *When Dad Hurts Mom,* 321.

living in abusive homes and witnessing violence can display the following behavioral problems:[9]

- Attention deficits
- Hyperactivity that interferes with learning and attention
- Learning delays
- Sleeping problems (nightmares, fear of sleep, bedwetting)
- Body pains (headaches, stomach problems and pains)
- Delays in language acquisition
- Poor academic performance
- Missing school often (truancy or sickness)
- Falling asleep in school
- Sibling rivalry or hierarchy.

A second reason for a victim to consider taking her children with her when leaving an abusive partner is that children who are in abusive homes *have a greater risk of being physically abused.* This child abuse can begin even before a child's birth. The narcissistic belief system of the abuser increases the chance for a woman to be abused when she is pregnant. If abuse is occurring in a relationship, pregnancy can increase the frequency or intensity of abuse.[10] There is great risk for the baby during this time, and many victims have claimed that the abuser hit them in the stomach when they were pregnant. Abusive men also may abuse their growing children. Bancroft suggests that 40 percent of abusive men carry their behavior pattern toward their spouse over onto other family members, and batterers have a higher rate of violating children's boundaries than nonbatterers.[11] Children, many times, in an attempt to protect their mothers, get in the way of the husband abusing his wife and receive the brunt of the violence.

Another reason for an abuse victim to take her children with her when she leaves her partner is that the *strong similarities in the behavior of abusers and pedophiles warrant removing children from abusive homes.* "Multiple studies demonstrated that the mothers of incest victims are likely to be battered by the perpetrator. Other studies indicate that daughters of batters have unusu-

9. Bancroft, *When Dad Hurts Mom,* 76, 145–46; Boston Medical Center (http://www.child-witnesstoviolence.org)

10. Burch and Gallup, "Pregnancy as a Stimulus for Domestic Violence," 243–47; Martin et al., "Changes in Intimate Partner Violence during Pregnancy," 201–10.

11. Bancroft, *When Dad Hurts Mom,* 53, 55.

ally high rates of incest victimization. These two sets of studies taken together suggest that exposure to batterers is among the strongest indicators of risk of incest victimization."[12]

While the studies do not suggest that all abusive men are pedophiles, the similarities between the two behaviors and high incidences of pedophilia by abusive men indicate that children in abusive homes are at greater risk of being sexually abused by their abusive parent, stepparent, or parent's partner. This evidence suggests that we should not always assume that the statement, "he abuses me but he wouldn't hurt the children," is true. Abuse victims must be encouraged and empowered to leave their spouse or have them removed. Abused women have the right and responsibility to protect their children and provide a peaceful home for them to grow and develop.

Finally, exposure to batterers *increases a child's chances of being involved in abusive relationships in the future.* Not all abusers were raised in abusive homes, and not all from abusive homes continue to abuse. Yet parents, the surrounding culture and media, and/or peer relationships or gangs can model abusive behavior. Children need to be removed from an environment that supports power and control over another and encouraged to develop compassion, love, and a sense of encouragement.

Victims must be open with their children about what they have experienced. Many of the abuse victims do not talk about the abuse with their children or families. Sometimes they are ashamed, and other times they believe that ignoring the problem may make it go away. Children, however, remember their experiences and try to process what they see and hear. They have questions that many of us wish to ask: "How can daddy be nice and then mean?" "Why did you stay with him knowing that he beats me?" "Why did you go back to daddy again?" "Are all people this cruel?" As Bancroft has written, "Avoiding the subject will not lessen their fear; in fact, children feel safer if they can talk to their mothers about how frightened they get, and discuss actions they might take next time their father erupts."[13]

Children need to know that what happened was wrong and unacceptable. If children do not learn to make distinctions between right and wrong, they will be more likely to practice the same type of manipulation when they become adults. Children need to hear from their parents that it was necessary for them to leave and that they will now be safe. They need to know that Mom is doing what is best for them by leaving Dad and trying to protect her family.

12. Bancroft and Silverman, *The Batterer as Parent*, 84.
13. Bancroft, *When Dad Hurts Mom*, 303.

When women leave their abuser, they provide the opportunity for the children to process and heal from the affects of domestic violence. Divorce or separation can be difficult and traumatic for children, so they need an environment in which they can discuss their feelings and what they have witnessed. Key elements that are helpful for children's healing from abuse are:[14]

- a close relationship with their mother
- a safe place to live
- a good relationship with their siblings
- a good connection to other loved ones, peers, and self
- an ability to talk and express their feelings openly
- freedom to release distressing feelings through
  - » crying
  - » raging
  - » laughing
- the ability to obtain good information about abuse.
- the power to
  - » think critically at teachable moments
  - » address the culture and media issues that support abuse
  - » define how they cope with fear and discouragement.

Victims and their children can heal together and form a united front so that they can approach their future and their abuser with confidence and courage.

Finally, victims must *work with an established domestic-violence support system.* There is no shame in asking for help or in receiving aid in order to become self-sufficient.

> Without consultation plans are frustrated but with many counselors they succeed. (Prov 15:22)

> A wise person listens to counsel. (Prov 12:15)

There is no shame in seeking advice from abuse-intervention counselors and advocates. Our government has provided our communities with grants, trainings, and programs to help domestic-violence victims become indepen-

14. Ibid., 269–70, 292–311.

dent and peaceful parents. Victims need to take advantage of abuse-survivors' support groups. These groups help women heal, forgive, find employment, practice nonviolent parenting, and find financial aid or rental assistance so that they do not have to return to their abuser in order to survive. Shelters, homes, centers, and women's groups provide a plethora of resources for abuse victims seeking help and support. Prevention is still the best medicine for abuse.

Churches Must Become Involved

Churches and other faith communities must also *encourage victims to protect their children*, even if it means being a single parent. Churches can help women who have been victims of abuse overcome the shame associated with being a single mother and can empower them to stand on their own and provide for their family. Single mothers struggle with a deep sense of shame and guilt from feelings that "I couldn't make my marriage work." Women who take a stand and leave or remove their dysfunctional spouses should be commended for their courage and desire to provide a peaceful and safe home for their children as well as for themselves. Jesus warns the disciples against "causing little ones to sin" (Matt 18:5–6). When we allow children to be exposed to violence and abuse, and do not try to protect them, we commit a great crime against God. Churches and ministries must stress that protecting children and encouraging them to "be children" is the desire of Jesus.[15]

Churches *must work with government and local agencies in order to provide victims with the best resources possible.* Many churches distrust outside agencies and believe that they will tear apart the family. In the introduction to this book, I reproduce a letter I received from Mary, a victims' advocate. She wrote in part: "In the past I had three clients return to their abusive homes because the batterer suddenly became religious, and they ended up getting marriage counseling . . . Then this past week I moved a domestic violence victim into another small neighboring town so that she could have some peace of mind, and one Pastor called another Pastor and they tracked her down and confronted her on her front lawn at 8:30 pm. Her interpretation of the contact was that she was a bad wife for leaving her husband . . ." Mary's e-mail indicates that it is the faith community that is complicating the problem of abuse in families. Churches can work with outside agencies to provide what they cannot: spiritual support. Women's groups and divorce-recovery ministries can support victims by reminding them that God loves them, and that they have a safe spiritual home. The children can develop relationships with

15. For a discussion of the Lukan text and challenge to act on behalf of children (Luke 18:15–17), see Clark, "Kingdoms, Kids, and Kindness," 235–48.

other children and see healthy, loving families worshipping God and practicing peace and forgiveness. Churches may also have access to financial aid and personal donors who can help the women provide for their families.

Youth-ministry leaders also have a great opportunity to work with young people in this area. Adolescents who are exposed to domestic violence many times will talk about it with their friends. When young people address the issue of violence occurring in their homes, youth-ministry leaders become mandatory reporters. Many youth ministers have kept the issue confidential, yet this continues the negative effect on the child. The longer young people are exposed to this behavior, the more they are damaged emotionally and spiritually. Rather than ignoring the problem, youth ministries must help teens and preteens address the problem and find safety. While the Bible says to honor father and mother, it also tells us that ignoring the cries of the oppressed distance us from God (Prov 21:13).

A college student once asked me what I had to do by law if someone told me that his or her father had been abusive. "What would happen to you legally if you did not tell?" he asked.

"Well, legally there are many issues and circumstances involved, but I do know that God would punish me if I did not help the person," I said. At the core of what we Christians do is the love of justice and truth that leads us to protect anyone from abuse and oppression. Christians must realize that children living in abusive homes are emotionally and physically at risk and must work to protect them.

Youth-ministry leaders should also keep the issue of domestic violence in mind when addressing issues such as rebellion against parents and sex outside of marriage. I have listened to speakers at youth rallies speak out about respecting parents. How does a child of abuse hear this statement? How does a child who has been sexually molested respond to a lesson about sex outside of marriage and about virginity? Children of domestic violence and abuse struggle with shame and guilt, and the way we approach these two topics is important if we want to minister to them. It is a good idea to assume that at least one teen listening to any sermon or devotional may be living in an abusive family. How we address these issues will affect how they see themselves and how they see God.

Abusers Must Be Called to Change

Since batterers have a tremendous affect on children, the process of repentance for an abusive spouse must include repentance to the children. First, abusers must be challenged to *keep an emotional distance from their families* until they are adequately progressing in batterer-intervention counseling. The temptation to manipulate and control will be hard to avoid, and it can only be overcome with intensive therapy and counseling. Children must be allowed to be children and no longer to be a part of the power-and-control cycle of abuse.

Second, batterers must be challenged to *provide financially for their wives or former wives and for their children*. While visitation rights may one day be granted, it is important that the batterers heal, and that their families grow and develop in a peaceful environment. It is not the victim's and children's fault that they are living as a single-parent family and trying to pay the bills and make ends meet. The abuser must take responsibility for his actions by providing them with financial help so that they can experience life free from violence and abuse.

Third, batterers must *support their wives in their own personal growth and development*. Their wives have a hard road ahead, and the abusive partner must back away and let them heal. The temptation recovering abusers face is to humiliate, criticize, and shame their wives; these strategies are still processes of control and manipulation. Abusers must encourage and empower their wives to be the best that they can be, but this may only come by letting them leave and grow, as they desire. An abuser should put his main focus on becoming a man of God rather than getting his family under his control.

Being a single parent should not be a curse; it should be a choice that involves the single parent and the faith community. Often if an abuser will not change, however, his wife may have no option other than divorce. Yet past studies and statistics have been used to enforce in many marriages the "keep-it-together-at-all-costs" mentality that has kept victims in abusive relationships. This mentality has not been healthy for either abuse victims or their children, because it links shame and divorce, and so deepens the shame that abuse victims already experience. (As has been mentioned already, the solution to saving failing marriages is not to encourage or to discourage divorce; the solution is to discourage and address dysfunction.) Given the shame that many abuse victims feel, if a victim becomes a single parent, the church can help her focus on herself and her family to rebuild self-esteem and peace.

The church can also give the victim and her family hope that they can develop spiritually and emotionally even though they are a single-parent family. Studies in Sweden suggest little difference in the cognitive ability, social adaptability, and personality development of children brought up in single-parent and two-parent homes.[16] The church can provide resources and a

16. Dahlberg, "The Parent-Child Relationship and Socialization in the Context of Modern Childhood," 128.

place of acceptance for children who have come out of abusive homes. Rather than condemning divorce, the faith community should address dysfunction. Rather than judging single-parent homes, the church should support them and offer help. Rather than feeling sorry for these children, the church can empower their parents to be compassionate, strong, and merciful.

If the church is in the position to work with the abusive parent, it can accept the batterer and call him to accountability. It can encourage the abuser to take responsibility for his actions and to provide for his family. He should pay for their temporary housing, counseling, and medical bills. While this places a tremendous strain on the abuser, the church can be there to encourage him and let him know that this is the just action and part of the repentance process. The church can support him in attending counseling and confessing his sins to his spouse or ex-spouse, to his children, and to other family members. The faith community can help him to change his behavior in order to become the compassionate and loving father that God has called him to be.

CHAPTER 8

ROADBLOCK 3: Am I Supposed to Be a Victim?

H AVE YOU EVER noticed that our society seems to focus on victims rather than oppressors or abusers? This may seem like an odd statement, but read the newspaper or listen to the news reports about crime. Notice how the headlines are presented:

- "*Woman Raped* by Stalker"
- "*Man Attacked* by Thief"
- "*Child Molested* by Father
- "*Thousands Killed* in Terrorist Attacks."

What is wrong with these statements? They do not give an accurate picture of the events. They are passive accounts of the story. The real issue should be addressed by blaming the rapist, thief, or molester rather than the victim. What if the headlines read differently?

- "*Man Stalks and Rapes* Woman"
- "*Thief Attacks and Brutally Beats* Man"
- "*Father Molests* Child"
- "*Terrorists Kill* Thousands."

Too often reports, investigations, and charges focus on the victim, not the offender. This is why we hear people ask questions that seem to accuse the victim: Why was she out at that time of night? Why was he in that part of town? Why didn't the child tell someone? Were these people in the wrong place at the wrong time?

Compassion for abused women is building across the continent, but we are still a society with deep habits of blaming victims. When people suffer misfortune, we jump to analyzing what they should have done differently: She should have fought back, she shouldn't have fought back; she was in an area where it wasn't wise to be walking; she didn't plan ahead; she didn't try hard enough or think fast enough . . . These judgments can tragically limit the support and compassion that an abused woman receives from her community . . . In addition to over-simplifying her options, blaming the mother has the effect of reinforc-ing the abusive man's own messages to her.[1]

Unintentionally these questions suggest that it is the victim's fault or choice to be raped, beaten, molested, or killed. Yet, the victim is not to blame. The abuser commits the crime and needs to be held accountable. Notice how many victims' services exist in our government programs. We help victims, but how often do we confront abusers? Are we afraid to address oppression, or do we have a preoccupation with victimization?

Lori and I attended a Portland-area domestic-violence intervention fund-raising dinner. The faith-based domestic-violence intervention group called ARMS (short for Abuse Recovery Ministry & Services) is an outstanding min-istry and has worked with both survivors and batterers throughout the Pacific Northwest. During the dinner a courageous woman gave her testimony about coming out of an abusive Christian marriage and helping her mother do the same. About twenty-five of us in the audience of four hundred plus gave her a standing ovation. Later a man gave his testimony of how the ministry of ARMS had confronted him and helped him go through a court-mandated program, repent of his abusive behavior, and reconcile with his wife and chil-dren. The man received a standing ovation from the whole audience. Lori looked at me and said, "That's odd; why didn't we do this for the survivor?" Fortunately when advocate and abuse survivor Nancey Murphy, the evening's presenter, stood up to speak, she very graciously asked us to all stand for the women who had had the courage to speak out and to come out of abusive relationships. Lori and I went home thinking how odd it was that we in the audience had initially supported the oppressor more than the oppressed.

I think that this example says something about our psyche. Why do we tend to criticize the victims and praise the oppressors?

- Maybe we resent being bullied.

- Maybe deep down we are afraid of the oppressors.

- Maybe we see victims as weak.

- Maybe we secretly want to be bullies and in control.

1. Bancroft, *When Dad Hurts Mom*, 313–14.

I have also observed these same fears in our nation's response to 9-11 in New York City. Those firefighters, police, and other rescuers who died in the Twin Towers, we call heroes. They were. But why do we feel compelled to call those ordinary folks in the Towers heroes as well? Aren't they victims? They went to work as people do every day and were killed by terrorists. Doesn't that make them victims? It doesn't lessen the loss, but for some reason we hesitate to call them victims. Is this a matter of semantics or a reflection of society's dislike for victims or for what it means to be victimized?

I experience the same fearful preoccupation with victims as I talk to Christians today and move around in the culture at large. For instance, one recent cultural phenomenon, Mel Gibson's *The Passion of the Christ*, reminded me how, for centuries, Christianity has been obsessed with the victimization, suffering, and pain of Jesus. While my wife and I appreciate Gibson's work as director, it seems that this movie is an example of how Christianity has become overly focused on the cross and on the victimization of Jesus Christ. The graphic display Jesus's suffering seemed to be overdone in the film, and at times I felt like I was watching a cross between *Braveheart* and *Rocky*. The movie suggests that Jesus suffered more than any other crucified individual, and it even took liberties to intensify the beatings, which seemed to move the audience (me included) to tears. It is important for us to understand the suffering of Jesus, but there is a reason why the Bible briefly tells the story of the crucifixion. There is a reason why the gospel writers did not dwell on the death and crucifixion of Jesus as much as they did on his life. He was a victim, and this was the age-old story of a God rejected by people and victimized by terrorists.

How Does Necrophilia Relate to Victimization?

Necrophilia is a preoccupation with or love of death. While it may have sexual overtones, it indicates a romantic notion of death or dead things. I feel that sometimes the church may be guilty of necrophilia. This may be a major cause for the victimization that I tend to see in our ministry to victims. Why necrophilia? Because the church has focused on the cross for centuries. It has been the emblem of Christianity. It has become the center of our preaching and a place for us to return to when we need to reflect on our spiritual lives.

I am a member of the Churches of Christ, which have a biblical tradition of celebrating communion every Sunday morning. Over the years people in my former churches have complained about the communion devotionals if they do not emphasize the death and suffering of Jesus. In communion talks there is a strong emphasis on Jesus's death and sacrifice as well as a feeling of remorse and sorrow when we take the emblems. We are reminded weekly that Jesus suffered for us. Sometimes communion talks will focus on the last few hours of Jesus's life and include a graphic description of the flogging, crucifixion, or beatings from the soldiers. I have heard speakers tell us that we should shed a tear or hang our head during this time. If we do not, something is wrong with us. So often these reminders cross the line and tell us, "We killed Jesus"—something that the Bible does not suggest. At times, communion becomes a funeral service, and if its not, people get concerned.

This same emphasis is in our Christian literature. What is the problem with Christianity, they ask? We are arrogant, proud, cocky, rebellious, or materialistic. What is the solution? We need a healthy dose of the cross to keep us in line. Many popular books have been written to call us back to the cross, which is supposed to represent who we are as Christians. We are reminded that those crosses on our necks are not real crosses.

- Real crosses are hard, painful, and shameful.
- Volumes of books have been written lamenting the fact that we have forgotten the value of the cross.
- We need to be reminded of the old rugged cross, the authors tell us.
- The cross keeps us in line, like a good switch.
- The cross humbles us and knocks us to our knees, like a good kick to the groin.
- The cross keeps us focused on our sin and its consequences, like that disappointing glance from mom or dad when we've done something bad.
- The cross is there to keep us from ever feeling too good about ourselves.
- The cross is a reminder that we are nothing, we are worthless, and we are worms (*for such a worm as I* . . .).
- DEATH, DEATH, DEATH . . .

Yet after all is said and done, we are supposed to find peace in the cross. God sent Jesus to die for us, and we should find comfort in the fact that Jesus received our beatings and death. He suffered for us so that we would not have to feel the wrath of God. Jesus and the cross are similar to the big brother who received the punishment that we deserved and then reminds us of that every week. What a thrilling thought! One time Jesus took my punishment and for the rest of my life, every week, someone reminds me of that. Every time I come to church, I am reminded that I should get a beating, but Jesus took it for me. I am reminded that I daily sin and kill Jesus. As a song that we sing states, "Does he still feel the nails every time I sin?"

Not only this, but I am also reminded that we are all sinners (despite what the Bible tells us), and that every day I commit a myriad of sins. There is nothing I can do to stop this. I can try, but ultimately I will sin each day. To think that I can stop sinning is seen as arrogance and pride. The cross then becomes my whipping post. I am told that the cross reminds me that I have a substitute for my punishment who continues to suffer every day for my and for our sins. Jesus is continually a victim, and every Sunday he is victimized. Not only is Jesus victimized, so are we. The story of the cross is told over and over again, and we are forced to feel the horror and sadness that the apostles only briefly mention in their writings and sermons. In fact, our modern "cross teachers" are more graphic than Matthew, Mark, Luke, and John felt they needed to be! If we do not grieve, we may feel unspiritual or arrogant. If we want hope, we are told that the cross is where we find it. Is it a wonder that critics of Christianity have sensed this victimization and spoken out against it?

In my past studies and meetings with atheists, Satanists, and philosophy students, I find that, as with Friedrich Nietzsche, Anton LaVey, and others, there is a distaste for Christianity. This distaste is not because we Christians conquer sin and love others, but it is because we try to overcome sin by claiming to be victims to it!

There is compelling evidence that we have been wrong. First, have you noticed that the Gospel writers did not feel the need to tell us all the graphic details of the crucifixion? Have you noticed that only one chapter of each gospel is devoted to the crucifixion story? What was their emphasis? Their emphasis was on the resurrection, not the crucifixion.

Imagine going to a funeral of someone who has died of cancer. When friends stand up to speak, how do they talk about the deceased? Do they say, "She lived a great life, but I want to talk about the agony she faced for six hours last week. I want to talk about her hair falling out, her screaming in pain, and her begging to die." In the eulogy people talk about her life, her accomplishments, and her courage. This was the purpose of the Gospels. The message of the gospel and resurrection brought hope, healing, forgiveness, power, and the work of the Holy Spirit—not guilt and depression.

But doesn't the Apostle Paul tell us that the cross is the "crux" of Christianity? Paul does speak of the cross and emphasizes that part of his ministry, but even more he discusses the resurrection. While his letters make many references to the cross, Paul's point is that the resurrection provides the power, hope, victory, and justice for life on this earth and for the next life. The cross is important, but *it should never overshadow the resurrection.*

This is what I believe we have missed. We are like the disciples on the road to Emmaus (Luke 24:14–32). This was the first sermon about Jesus given to an outsider after the resurrection. What was the lesson? Jesus was killed, and the tomb is empty. That was it! No hope, no joy, and no power. Yet Jesus revealed himself to them in the breaking of bread. In the breaking of bread and the teaching of Scripture, they recognized the risen Jesus rather than the dead Jesus. It was the resurrected Jesus that caused their hearts to burn (Luke 24:32)!

And so it is with us. We are so overcome with grief, shame, and sadness in Jesus's death that we can't see the living Lord. Communion and Bible study have little life because we only see the cross and an empty tomb with questions and a handful of testimonies. In our centuries of focus on the crucifixion and the cross, we have neglected the resurrection. In fact, it seems that we have completely ignored the resurrection. The very stage of the story that brought hope, healing, forgiveness, vindication, and freedom became a footnote to the story. The resurrection is the heart of the gospel and should be the focus of the Christian faith. It makes Christianity different from any other religion. It illustrates the impossible and proves the power of God.

I don't want anyone to misunderstand what I am saying. I am not devaluing the cross, suffering, and death of Jesus. Those actions show the love and passion that God has for all of us. I am not trying to minimize the sacrifice Jesus made for all humans. I am not despising the story of the passion of the Christ. I am trying to deflate what *we have done* with the crucifixion, and inflate what *we should be doing* with the resurrection. It is my contention that our fixation on the death, pain, and suffering has caused us to neglect the very power of the gospel. It seems that we have become disoriented because of our fixation on the cross. Our symbol should be an empty tomb!

> In him you were also circumcised, in the putting off of the sinful nature, not with a circumcision done by human hands but with the circumcision done by Christ, when you were buried with him in baptism and *raised with him through your faith in God's power, who raised him from the dead.* When you were dead in your sins and in the uncircumcision of your sinful nature *God made you alive with Christ, he forgave us all our sins* . . . (Col 2:11–13)

After the publication of my first book, in which the comments above also appeared, I found them met with either joy or hostility. Some suggested that I was trying to diminish the suffering of Christ because I was trying to make the gospel fit "abuse psychology." Others shared with me that they have felt "beat up" for years and welcomed a heavier focus on the resurrection. However, I came to realize that the problem is not the cross but how we use it. I have had a couple theologians challenge me on this, and others smile and acknowledge that the Eastern Church taught us to focus on the resurrection. However, when we discuss this over coffee, we all acknowledge that the cross has been overemphasized for many years.

One Sunday morning, shortly after we planted the Agape Church of Christ, we were discussing the suffering of Jesus/God. Since my sermons have become mostly dialogue with this new church, one of the young women asked how God could understand the suffering and abuse that women face in this world. At that point it connected. I shared with her that in the humiliation of the cross, Jesus identifies with those who are humiliated and suffer. They, like Jesus, know the pain, shame, and guilt. Therefore Jesus becomes their model for life not by suffering but by the hope of resurrection, justice, and a new life. Abusers, however, need to identify with Jesus's suffering through empathy for their victims, repentance, and self-denial.

Abuse Victims and Victimization

In the previous two chapters, we have discussed two major roadblocks to healing for domestic-violence victims: First, an emphasis on avoiding divorce rather than addressing dysfunction in marriage prevents victims from leaving their partners even when their safety is at risk. Second, an assumption that a two-parent home is always better for children than a single-parent home prevents victims of domestic violence and their children from fleeing their abusive spouse. A third major roadblock to the healing of victims of domestic violence is *victimization*. If a woman who is abused comes to worship in some of our churches, the image of a victim is continually before her. If suffering is our main calling, then her calling is to suffer at home. If Jesus suffered and won, then her victory comes through her submission to an abusive husband and looking for a victory through this suffering. If Jesus was helpless and a victim of sin, then she is also helpless and a victim of sin. If we are unworthy, sinful, or flawed humans, then she is even more so. Remember, her husband has told her how unworthy she is. If he attends church with her, then his role as a "good Christian husband," is to keep her in line. Her cross is to obey him. "The glorification of Jesus' suffering also leads to a theological sadism and an image of God as a violent, angry, sadistic father. When the cross becomes the goal of love, love is distorted and perverted."[2]

A suffering Savior is an incomplete savior. Like the men on the road to Emmaus, we only see a dead Jesus and empty tomb. Victims see a victimized Savior and an empty tomb that only causes questions. They will find Scriptures that support their suffering and that suggest they can serve their tyrant spouse into salvation. They will take to heart the sermons that give them a sense of false hope that they can overcome abuse by patient submission. They will *amen* when preachers tell them that abuse is their cross and that they must carry it alongside Jesus. They truly love God, but they believe that if they could be more submissive (or Christlike in their eyes), they could save their marriages. They feel that God has called them to suffer, and their abusive marriage is their cross. As Jesus told the disciples to pick up their crosses daily (Luke 9:23–27), so daily a Christian woman living with domestic violence shoulders the burden of shame, rejection, abuse, and guilt. She feels that spirituality is *overfunctioning* and outserving the *underfunctioning* spouse. She is like Hagar sent back to abusive Sarah. She is like David returning to violent Saul. She is like Tamar begging Amnon, her half brother and rapist, to take her back.

Oksana had called to tell me that she wanted anger-management training for her husband, Victor.

"Why don't you have him call me?" I said.

"Well, he really doesn't think he has a problem," she said. "He says that I am the cause of this."

"Oksana, when you told me earlier that there was abuse, what did you mean?"

She immediately responded with, "Pushing, shoving, holding me down, verbally abusing me, pulling my hair."

"Has he ever hit you or assaulted you?"

"Yes," she said. "I know this is not right, but I have been living with this for eight years. His son verbally abuses me now. My family wants me to get out."

"Oksana, God does not want you to be treated this way. You deserve to be respected and loved by your husband."

"Yes I know. I love God. I go to Applegate Community Church, and Victor and I heard a great sermon about marriage yesterday. I really feel I can commit to this and make it work. I can be a better wife—"

"Hey, Oksana," I interrupted. "God does not expect you to stay in a marriage where you are being abused. Applegate Community Church has not been

---

2. Gill-Austern, "Love Understood as Self-Sacrifice and Self-Denial," 308.

open to what we teach about abuse and marriage. The Bible teaches that your husband is breaking the marriage vows by abusing you. Your family and your Lord love you and want you to be safe, as well as the children."

"I know," she said. "It's hard."

"You can come in and talk anytime. We won't force you to leave, and we will just listen. But we want you to be safe. God wants you to be safe!"

Oksana was like many other women with whom we talk. She believed that her safety and self-respect were to be priorities, but her faith community reminded her that being a Christian meant being a victim. Somehow they had convinced her that by serving and taking it on the chin, she and God would be able to change a violent and controlling man. She was also wrongly taught that God expected her to be a victim and to suffer abuse at the hands of a man who did not love her.

Children can also be affected by this victimization. If they have witnessed abuse, they have learned that bullying is a means to get what they want. They have also seen that the abused find a way to survive by being good and catering to the abuser. In the church, submission will be viewed as a means of survival rather than as a willing attitude of love and sacrifice. Serving may become a compulsion for children of abuse, because they do it out of fear rather than love. They will also have a view that God is powerless to help victims. And they will become angry as they wrestle with a God who saves Shadrach, Meshach, and Abednego from the fiery furnace, but who does not respond to the cries of their mother or to their own cries to be saved from their fiery and abusive parent. They will learn that bullies must be served, abusive parents must be supported, and victims receive no power from God to protect themselves. Addressing abused mothers, Lundy Bancroft writes:

> Children pick up on the threats, whether implied or explicitly stated, that are communicated by the abusive man's explosive outbursts and aggressive body language, and your flinching or frightened reactions. The research on children's exposure to partner abuse shows that they are aware of much more of their father's violence than the parents think they are, and can sometimes describe incidents in detail that both Mom and Dad didn't think the child even saw. These experiences are scary for children. They worry that their mother will get hurt, perhaps so severely that she won't be able to look after them. They lie awake in bed staring into the dark or wake up later from nightmares. And they worry that someday he will turn his violent behavior toward them . . .[3]

3. Bancroft, *When Dad Hurts Mom*, 34–35.

Abusers and Victimization

Batterers who come to a church that has this "victim theology" will also have a hard time healing. First, abusers do *feel that they are victims*, and that others are causing the unjust suffering. If they have been served with a restraining order or mandated to a batterer-intervention program, they will feel victimized by "the system." Churches with a victim- and shame-based theology will not be able to confront the abusers and call them to accountability.

Second, abusers *may become predatory* in a church community and look for women who are encouraged to stay victims. The reason many predatory ministers and church leaders have been able to practice pedophilia, physical and sexual abuse, or power and control over members is that they are in an environment that reinforces submission. Members trust these leaders and seek advice, comfort, and guidance from them. Empowerment helps victims become strong and self-confident. Victimization keeps them dependent on strong personalities. Abusers will sense this and victimize others. Abusers need to be in an environment that promotes justice. This means that the community of faith has the responsibility to help the abuser overcome his nature and tendency to reoffend. Faith communities must remind abusers that they are expected to change, and that the gospel calls them to be transformed into loving, peaceful, and compassionate men.

Churches can help abusers by accepting that victims' vindication can result in a positive feeling. Being overcome with anger and vengeance is unhealthy, and understanding victims' desire for vindication can bring a sense of awareness to those who victimize others. The community of faith should uphold morality by reflecting a sense of vindication for victims. Abusers should be accepted and loved but also reminded that they are not the victims, and that they need to change. The community can be a source of tough love for abusers by expressing anger for their actions and sins. This anger will not be motivated by personal pain but by a sense of moral justice, holiness, and spiritual devotion. The faith community can be stern yet loving.

> No longer will individual victims of wrongdoing be free to pursue individual—and thus unpredictable and socially dangerous—revenge. Rather the community will, as it were, take on the personae of victims and act in their names—act in the regular, procedural, proportional, and predictable manner that we associate with the rule of law.[4]

Abusers can feel a sense of stability in a community that loves them yet condemns their actions. But they must be willing to change and face the

4. Murphy, *Getting Even*, 20.

long road of pain, suffering, and struggle that is necessary to modify their abusive behavior.

Was or Is God a Victim?

Much of what I have written may disturb readers who see Jesus as a victim. Was Jesus a victim? Has God ever been a victim? I think that the answer to these questions begins with a definition of a victim. First, a *victim suffers unjustly*. What happens to them is not their fault or their choice. Victimization is not punishment. The victim receives pain and suffering that is undeserved. What is happening is unfair and should be stopped. Second, a *victim is not in control of the situation*. Victims have no power to start, stop, or change the amount of suffering. While they may feel a false sense of control in the cycle of domestic violence, it is the abuser who is practicing the control. Victims many times are helpless and powerless to change the situation. Finally, *victims suffer because of the works of evil*. There is no value in what is happening to them. God is not punishing them or acting upon them. They suffer because evil is active. Victims cannot make something good come out of their suffering, because nothing good has been in their suffering from the start. A victim is being affected by evil.

While in this unjust world of suffering, victims survive by reframing their view of reality. If one is victimized and cannot change the situation, then one will change the outlook. Victims will have to believe that God has a *purpose for their suffering*. Since God is in control of all things, God has a plan for this process. God is seen as one who ordains this suffering. The victim is to *endure* this suffering and *find meaning to* the suffering. Like Job, victims assume that God has brought evil upon them.

> Yahweh gave, Yahweh took away, blessed is the name of Yahweh. (Job 1:21b)

Unfortunately, Job was not able to read the beginning of the biblical book that bears his name, as we have, so he was not aware of the war in heaven between God and Satan. Because he was suffering, his perspective was that God had brought suffering upon him. In fact, in the biblical story, Job never even acknowledges that Satan exists. However, it is Satan who brings evil on Job, but Job is trying to find meaning *to* his suffering rather than meaning *in* his suffering.

The experiences of suffering, to those who try to find meaning *to* suffering, become a means to greater good and have an appearance of goodness.

With this comes the desire for or the glorification of suffering. While this may be a method of survival, it ignores the basic premise that victims suffer unjustly due to the work of Satan and evil choices by other humans. Suffering is experienced, accepted, and many times expected by victims. "Sexual and domestic violence are forms of involuntary suffering. Neither serves any useful purpose; neither is chosen by the victim; neither is ever justified. Yet both cause great suffering for large numbers of people."[5]

Finding meaning to suffering is a passive form of spirituality and a passive resistance to evil in the world. The Christian, with this view, is not able to oppose various forms of evil or personal injustice. The Christian only learns to accept all things that happen as if they are by the hand of a mysterious God. With this view, suffering is expected and accepted as part of our spiritual growth.

Suffering that is chosen is not victimization. A person who chooses suffering for a greater good is not a victim. In the book of Hosea, God chooses to take unfaithful Israel back as a wife (Hos 2:14–23). God chooses to be faithful in the covenant even when the people of Israel had broken the covenant and were punished. God also chooses to initiate a new covenant with those who had rejected the Creator. Yet in the later book of Malachi, God's people again turn away and dishonored God (Mal 1:6). In Malachi, God had called them to repentance and warned them to change their ways. God continually initiates relationships with humans, knowing that this might bring suffering. Yet this was by choice. God was not a victim because the Lord always has the ability and right to respond as the Lord chooses.

When the disciple Peter felt the need to fight in order to defend Jesus from those who had come to arrest him, Jesus said, "Put your sword back in its place . . . Do you think I cannot call on my Father who will at once put more than twelve legions of angels at my disposal" (Matt 26:52–53)? Jesus made the choice to suffer. He willingly and knowingly chose to die. While the Romans and the Judean religious leaders felt that they had victimized Jesus, the gospels defend the Son of God and suggest that he willingly chose to suffer. The Holy Spirit also enters humans, knowing that they can choose to go with or against the will of God. While it is possible for humans to quench or to grieve the Holy Spirit (Isa 63:10; Eph 4:30; 1 Thess 5:18), the Spirit is never a victim.

The suffering of God was not victimization. God was not powerless even though this suffering was unjust and the result of evil. Throughout the Bible, God is in control but chooses not to act at times. When God decides to punish, God punishes. God sometimes makes a conscious choice to be abused,

5. Fortune, "The Transformation of Suffering," 143.

because a greater purpose or plan is involved. God also made a conscious choice to judge the wicked after the suffering. Jesus likewise made the conscious choice to suffer by being humiliated on the cross. Again, God is not a victim but God willingly chose to suffer.

Abuse victims, however, do not have the choice to suffer. I have heard many people say that battered wives must want to be victims, which is why they return to their abusers. This is not true. They return to their abusers because they are coerced, manipulated, and afraid. Their abuser doesn't say, "Come home so I can hit you again." Their abuser promises to change. They choose to return because they believe he will change. They are victims because the abuser lies and continues to control them. They are victims because they do not deserve to be abused. They are victims because they are not in control. They are victims because of evil. Many times they are victims because they are afraid to leave their relationship. Their suffering is unjust and angers God. It is wrong for us to compare their suffering to Jesus's suffering! While Jesus understands their pain, Jesus does not approve of their suffering. God has always been a God who protects and vindicates the weak, poor, oppressed, and afflicted. God expects the church to address this issue.

How Does the Resurrection Change This Approach?

If we make the resurrection our main focus, our views of sin and spiritual growth change. First, we realize that while we live in a fallen world, we are born again into a *risen kingdom*. The kingdom of God is a place of resurrection, victory, celebration, and hope. Paul states that the kingdom, "is righteousness, peace, and joy in the Holy Spirit" (Rom 14:17). The kingdom is a place where God's justice and mercy should reign. Second, rather than guilt, shame, and sadness, the church should become a place of *healing, forgiveness, and hope*. Victims can be protected and supported. We can empower them to be strong. The Spirit gives victims power and courage to transform their lives as well as the lives of their family. Victims are not told to carry their cross but to rise up and break free from captivity. The church must act by the Spirit and provide that hope, peace, and empowerment to women victims.

Abuse Victims and the Resurrection

How does the resurrection affect abuse victims? First, it gives them a sense of *empowerment*. The same God who raised Jesus from the dead can also transform the lives of women who come to us and are bruised, emotionally scarred, humiliated, and overcome with guilt and shame. They are encouraged when they hear that God wants them to be safe and strong. They do not have to be slaves in a marriage or relationship that brings violence, guilt, and manipulation. They are to be loved as humans made in the image of God, their Creator.

Second, the resurrection provides *freedom* for victims. The resurrected Savior illustrates that his death and suffering on the cross were not the end of Christianity. The new life and victory over the Savior's enemies illustrates that the church is to have a ministry of power and hope. Victims are not meant to live in guilt, suffering, and shame. They are to be free and live in safety, treated with love, compassion, and respect. They are to experience justice, not humiliation. If they choose to be married they are to be respected and loved.

Finally, the resurrection provides hope that victims *can forgive*. Through time, healing, and validation, victims can one day forgive those who abused them. They do not have to live the rest of their lives with anger, bitterness, and guilt. They are not forced to forgive, but they can one day make that choice. They have the right to expect the abuser to repent, to be accountable, and to compensate them for their suffering and unjust treatment. They have the chance to move forward in their lives and allow the healing process to continue.

Batterers and the Resurrection

The resurrection tells batterers that the risen Savior may be their enemy. *They need to repent.* Jesus has risen from the dead and is the judge of those who oppose the will of God. Batterers can no longer hide behind a religious façade and claim that their wives are to "submit to their husbands" unquestionably. They learn that it is not their submissive wives or the "love of a good woman" that will change them. It is their conscious decision to change and be like Jesus. As illustrated earlier in this book, they cannot expect their wives to be slaves to a marriage covenant. Those who abuse their spouses are sinning against their families and against God. The resurrection brings a sense of judgment and accountability for their actions. God is the God of the victim and is one who calls the abuser to change his ways or face wrath and judgment. As in the past, so today God confronts those who oppress others through the prophets and the faith community. Batterers must acknowledge their sin and begin the process of repentance.

Second, the resurrection means that *abusers can change*. Paul told the early Christians at Corinth: "And such were some of you, but you were washed, you were sanctified, you were justified in the name of the Lord Jesus Christ and by the Spirit of our God" (1 Cor 6:11).

The first letter to the church at Corinth is a beautiful letter from a church leader to a congregation struggling with sin. Paul reminded the Corinthians that they were to be in Christ, and that they had the hope of being, and were expected to be, the type of people that God had called them to be. The conversion of Saul of Tarsus is an example of how the resurrected Jesus confronted and converted a violent man, who later became an apostle (Acts 9:1–19). Saul's conversion came with a price (Acts 9:16), but it was also a second chance at life.

Family and Friends and the Resurrection

Those who are close to victims or abusers must also know that the resurrection gives them a sense of hope in facing domestic violence. It is frustrating trying to help a family member or friend leave an abusive relationship, but it is helpful to understand that this is a slow process. Just as maturity is a process, so is healing. I have held men and women who weep over their daughters, sisters, mothers, or friends who have returned to an abuser. They have listened and have sacrificed hours of time rescuing the victim and her children, only to see the victim return to the troubling situation. They have visited her and seen the bruises. They have tried to call her on the phone, only to be cut off. They have initiated contact, only to be ignored. They have been criticized for being too nosey. They mean well. They love her and have invested tremendous emotional, financial, and physical strength into helping her. They weep because they feel helpless. They are angry, confused, and tired. They want to give up. While their pain is not the same as the victim's, they still suffer. They love her and want what is best for her and the children. They have listened to her and been there for her, and at times they feel used. Yet, they still are called to act as if they love her abusive partner.

The resurrection provides hope. The resurrection tells them that *God is still working.* Just as Jesus rose from the dead, so the hope of resurrection is that their loved one will one day leave her deathlike surroundings. She is overcome with fear and is confused, but all their efforts are not in vain. Just as God sent prophet after prophet over the centuries, so they send her message after message over time. Some heeded the prophets and changed. Some victims of abuse finally hear their families and friends and leave for good.

God endured because someone would hear the call. Someone in another generation would respond. The call of God is constant, and someone eventually hears and responds. Family and friends of an abuse victim can endure with patience and hope, knowing that someday she may leave, or someday one of her children may break the cycle. The resurrection provides hope concerning the patience of God to transform lives one at a time.

Victim theology is bad theology. The church has too often preached the bad news rather than the good news. We have forgotten that the story did not end at the cross or the tomb. We have forgotten that Jesus is the risen Lord, not the dead rebel. We have forgotten that the center of the Apostle's preaching was that God did not abandon Jesus in the grave, not that Jesus was forsaken on the cross. While we were focusing on the tragic death of Jesus, we forgot to show the hope, healing, and justice in the resurrection. Maybe this is why we have shrugged our shoulders rather than stretched out our arms. The risen Lord calls for justice for victims.

CHAPTER 9

Is the Church among
the Prophets?

How should the church respond to domestic violence and abuse? The first few chapters of this book discussed how the church has many times failed to protect victims and to call abusers to accountability. I have suggested that this is due to our theology concerning marriage, parenting, and the resurrection. I have also suggested that the faith community has been guilty of ignoring or avoiding the issue of abuse.

"Do you speak Russian?" I said in Russian as I caught Alexander passing by. (Alexander was a minister at a Russian church. I had met him at a community event and approached him afterward).

"*Da*," he affirmed, smiling.

"Alexander, man, am I glad to meet you! I am Ron Clark, the guy who called you on the telephone last month about abuse training for Russian ministers. I finally am glad to put a face with the name."

"Yes. I remember the call," he said as he slowly backed away from me.

Leaning forward I said, "Hey, I know you are busy, but I would like to meet with you for coffee or a soda sometime. I would like to talk about a training for Russian-speaking ministers to address abuse issues in their congregations."

"Well, Dr. Clark, you see, we Russian ministers all have full-time jobs outside the church. We do not have the privilege of getting paid by our congregations to preach. I am a mechanic by trade, and I have limited time to do my ministry. In fact, you will find that most Russian ministers have the same problem. We would rather spend our time teaching lost people who need Jesus," he said as he handed me his card. "I do still have your card. Thank you."

"I understand, Alexander, and I hope that we can meet sometime," I said smiling as we parted.

I understand that ministers are busy. They are constantly bombarded with new techniques to *better their ministries*. With Alexander's comment, I didn't know whether to be insulted or simply to accept that he is a busy man trying to be nice to one of the many salesmen that these ministers have to face.

Two issues that Alexander mentioned should be addressed. First, the issue of *evangelism* was mentioned in Alexander's response. He felt that dealing with domestic-violence issues may not be part of evangelism. Most ministers struggle to define *evangelism* but suggest that we should be doing it. Church-growth texts and classes teach ministers to be preachers in the community but not to be involved in local activism or community work. We are told that it distracts us from the work of the gospel of Jesus. Does evangelism only mean preaching to people about Jesus? Is evangelism preaching only to those who are *lost*? Can evangelism involve family or social-justice issues? According to Alexander, teaching men to be compassionate with their wives is not evangelism. Equally, social-justice issues, such as the oppression of the weak, of children, or of women do not fall under his definition of *evangelism*.

Evangelism means *preaching a good message*. It is interesting that the first sermon Jesus gave in the synagogue was a good message that involved social justice. Luke wrote that when Jesus was given the scroll of Isaiah, he found the place where it was written and read:

> The Spirit of the Lord is upon me, who has anointed me to preach good news to the poor, sent me to announce freedom for the captives and give sight back to the blind, to release those who have been wounded, and to announce the year of the Lord's favor. (Luke 4:18–19)

After Jesus read this, he told the congregation that the Scripture was fulfilled that day in their presence. Jesus was placing an emphasis on his ministry and on those who were to receive the good news. The recipients of this good news were the poor, blind, oppressed and those freed from captivity. His lesson seems to be a theme that carried throughout Luke and Acts. When John the Baptist was about to die, he sent two of his disciples to see if Jesus was the Messiah. At that moment Jesus was healing and curing the sick, blind, and demon possessed. What was Jesus's response to the Baptist?

> Go and proclaim to John what you have seen and heard. The blind see again, the lame walk, the lepers are cleansed, the deaf hear, the dead are raised, the good news is preached to the poor, and blessed is anyone who is not repulsed by me. (Luke 7:22)

Luke's gospel and Acts were written to a community that needed to practice their ministry with outcasts. These outcasts included the poor, the weak, the sick, widows, children, Gentiles, Samaritans, and oppressed. Luke's gospel highlighted Jesus's work among the poor and oppressed in the community. He was known as the friend of sinners and tax collectors (5:30–31; 7:34). In Luke 4:18–19 and 7:22, the recipients of the *good news* are the poor and oppressed. Part of following Jesus meant accepting the ministry that he practiced. Evangelism meant bringing the good news to the poor, the outcasts, and the oppressed.

If evangelism means bringing good news to the oppressed, doesn't it include addressing spousal and child abuse? Shouldn't the church be concerned about domestic violence? Even more, if 25 percent of women in America have been physically abused,[1] how many people could we reach if we began to address domestic violence? If thousands of women in America are abused every year, how many of them need to know that Jesus wants to help them? If so many men abuse women, shouldn't we be calling them to repentance? Can evangelism involve telling victims and abusers that the kingdom of God is a place of peace, healing, justice, and hope?

A second issue that Alexander, the Russian pastor, mentioned involves those *lost people who need Jesus*. So the question arises, what should we do with those in the church who are being abused? If we save the lost who are abused, what do we do with them once they are part of our congregations? Are they supposed to be content with being *saved*? This has been much of the problem with the faith community and abuse. Women have come to Jesus for healing, have been baptized into Christ, and then are expected to stay in their abusive relationships. They are freed from the slavery of sin and abuse, but then they are expected to pick up their cross and stay prisoners. While their ministers and leaders are out *saving the world*, victims are physically and spiritually dying at home. Abuse victims who attend church have indicated that they feel as if God is unconcerned about their suffering. I meet many people who have walked away from God because they have grown up in a religious family where the father was abusive. My own father was raised in a conservative church family where there was alcohol and physical abuse, and he later became an atheist. He died not believing in God and never having heard a sermon that I preached. I saw the tension he continually faced over his childhood abuse issues and religion. I have come to regret that he linked the church's apathy about abuse with a notion that God is apathetic about abuse.

All people need Jesus. Jesus came to preach good news to the poor and oppressed. Evangelism means that we practice Jesus's ministry by bringing freedom and justice to all people who are oppressed. We call this social justice.

1. Stark and Flitcraft, "Spouse Abuse."

We live in a world where corporations, such as Starbucks, clearly define their commitment to social justice, but where the professing evangelical church seems to have forgotten this issue. Even worse, we have placed domestic abuse in a separate category (women's issues) from other broader, societal justice issues and have removed it from our social-justice language.

Social justice is evangelism. Social justice requires courage. It involves confronting the abusers, oppressors, and power structures that humiliate and control others. It also involves comforting those who have been oppressed and abused. It is not about being a hero; it is about being a prophet, a friend, and a representative of God. It is about letting people know that a prophet/church has been among them (Ezek 2:5). This is not about condemning; it is about telling people that God knows what is going on. Living prophetically gives a sense of validation to victims and of rebuke to abusers.

How Is the Church Prophetic?

Jesus the Prophet

If the church is going to be evangelistic, it must be like Jesus. If the church is going to be like Jesus, it must be prophetic. The Jesus in Luke's gospel was prophetic in that he called his earliest disciples to practice social justice. Luke 1:3 tells us that this gospel was written to Theophilus. This means that the letter was addressed to a noble Gentile (possibly a Christian) or to the Christian community. Luke's intention was to reinvestigate the story of Jesus and confirm what they had been taught.

Jesus the prophet challenged those in power to attend to the needs of victims. Jesus did this directly by challenging the religious leaders and wealthy elite to open their hearts to the rest of humanity. Jesus also does this indirectly in Luke's gospel as every generation experiences the parables, stories, and lessons that lift up the poor and criticize those who look down on them.

The Prophets of Old and New

Traditionally, prophets are seen as individuals who were crazy, were magicians, or were isolated from their communities. Many television shows concerning Jesus of Nazareth display John the Baptist as a loud, confrontational, and erratic preacher. Others see the prophets as fortune-tellers. In the ancient world, prophets were equated with mystics, fortune-tellers, magicians, and diviners. The Israelite prophets were described by their character and work for Yahweh. They held a deep conviction that they were called by Yahweh and brought a message directly from the Lord. Their prophecies began with, "This is what Yahweh says," and many times ended with, "declares Yahweh." Their courage and conviction was based not in themselves but in their calling from God.

When Amos and Micah prophesied about the abuse of the poor, it was something that they saw daily. When Jeremiah challenged the people to help the children and women of his day, he was speaking of what he saw in the streets. The judgment from Yahweh was the revelation, but the description was of crimes seen firsthand. The prophets of Israel and Judah usually preached what others already knew, but they did it with authority and conviction. They preached not only what people saw, but also what Yahweh saw. They were sent to tell the leaders that God saw what was happening and was expressing either judgment or pleasure.

Just as Jesus called his disciples to respond to what they had seen, so we as the new prophets are called to respond to the injustices and sins of our neighborhoods. Those of us who have learned to turn our heads to the injustices of society have also learned to turn our hearts away from the pain and anguish that God expresses to us in the Scriptures. The Bible reveals to us that abuse, oppression, and humiliation are unacceptable to the one who has created all of us in the divine image. Modern prophets are men and women who have an encounter with God and with evil.

How Does the Church Become Prophetic?

Churches have the unique opportunity to be prophetic in many areas of social justice. If the church believes that it is the arms and hands of Jesus, then it has the responsibility to go where Jesus went. It has the responsibility to see what God sees. It has the responsibility to speak what God wants spoken and to preach what Jesus preached. If Jesus preached freedom for the captives, then the church must preach the good news of freedom to those who are caught in domestic violence and abuse. Our attempts to build churches like Christian malls for Jesus, to travel afar to do revivals, and to build schools as fortresses for our children have been noble but have not fully reflected the passion and heart of God for the little people. We have tried to create empires of power for God rather than kingdoms of justice for the Prince of Peace. We have been prophetic in the sense that we speak our mind but not in the sense that we represent the mind of Christ.

If the church is going to be prophetic, it must be like Jesus. When we observe the ministry of Christ, we see that his ministry involved preaching and healing. The preaching of Jesus was meant to teach the good news of

God. Jesus informed the world that God had come to enact justice, mercy, and judgment upon sin and darkness. But Jesus also healed the sick and demon possessed. By healing and casting out demons, Jesus was confronting the powers of darkness and showing us that Satan was defeated. While we often try to debate whether miraculous power exists, and whether the casting out of demons happens in churches today, we forget that Jesus confronted all forms of evil. The disciples also were part of the fall of Satan in their ministry (Luke 10:17–19). Who of us feel called to be responsible for causing Satan to fall?

Jesus told the disciples, as well as us today, that he has defeated Satan and that we can trample on evil. We have been sent to confront evil and attack Satan in our ministries. The spirits submit to us if we are doing what God wants, and our ministries must confront evil on every front. This evil is not limited to sickness. When I look around my neighborhood, it is not cancer, leprosy, or blindness that I see gripping my neighbors. It is pornography, abuse, oppression, adultery, drugs, and alcoholism that are ripping people apart. Regardless of my theology on miraculous works in the church, I have to acknowledge that Jesus has given us the power to defeat these forms of evil. Does the church believe this?

Awareness

The church must create awareness by preaching, teaching, and speaking out concerning domestic violence. This means that the church must look to its leaders, especially those who carry the role of prophet, which are our preachers. They are the ones who must first have the encounter with God and open their eyes. They see the problem, but they have not addressed it. Awareness cannot happen unless the preachers of our churches alert us to the problem. This will involve three steps.

First, preachers *must acknowledge that there is a problem*. Acknowledgement means that we state that it is a problem. We do not make excuses for the violence, we do not ignore it and hope that it goes away, and we do not justify it. Acknowledgement means that we call it what God calls it: evil. Domestic violence is evil, and it is not the work of God but of Satan and of people choosing to do evil. As Jeffrey Means suggests, we must acknowledge that abuse is not only a sin but a great evil upon our land. "One of the few places evil has been consistently mentioned has been within communities of faith. At the same time, the church and religiously committed individuals have tended to leave evil unacknowledged as part of their own worlds and to ignore and deny the depth of evil's impact on people. When evil has been acknowledged, it too frequently is pushed outside."[2]

If preachers would communicate that domestic violence is evil, then the congregation would listen. Those who are victims would know that they are not to blame, and abusers would be called to repent. The church must acknowledge that abuse is a sin and a work of evil.

Second, preachers *must learn about this problem.* One of the biggest frustrations that domestic-violence service providers communicate with me about churches is that the leaders do not know how to work with those involved in abuse. Too often abusers manipulate counselors, ministers, and church leaders because they are not prepared to work with them. A pedophile goes before a congregation and says he's sorry for his sins, and the church assumes that he is cured and will not reoffend. An abuser confesses abusing his wife and children and states that it only happened once, and the church fully believes him. Yet the same congregation chides victims because they just, "can't get over it and get on with their lives." Church members push victims to forgive and forget as they themselves have. Yet they do not live in the same house with the abuser. In order to work with victims, their children, and abusers, we preachers and ministers must be aware of the issues present in the home. We live in a time when access to resources is easy, and information is readily available.

Finally, once preachers have acknowledged the problem and learned about the issues, they should *preach and teach about God and domestic violence.* The Bible is full of both stories and instructions about domestic violence. Narratives include the story of Dinah (Genesis 34), the account of the Levite and his concubine (Judges 19), and the story of Tamar and Amnon (2 Samuel 13). Instructions include regulations against uncovering family nakedness (Deuteronomy 27) and against child sacrifice (Leviticus 20) as well as codes of conduct for Christian households (Ephesians 5; Colossians 3; 1 Peter 3). Ministers have a great opportunity, given by God, to bring a text before the congregation and illuminate the issues of violence in the ancient world as well as today. God has spoken, in many of these texts, to the community concerning intimate-partner violence and abuse. Biblical writers and prophets illustrate God's judgment toward abusers and protection for victims.

According to victims, the sermon is one of the most encouraging ways to inform them that God grieves over their suffering. I have heard some abuse-intervention advocates grieve over the fact that their minister will not publicly denounce abuse. Some say that their minister alludes to, refers to, or touches

2. Means, *Trauma & Evil,* 9.

on the topic. But I have heard very, very few tell me that their minister has given a full sermon on domestic violence and the gospel. Is it because so many ministers are male? Is it because this has been seen as a women's issue?

> Domestic violence and sexual abuse should not be made as "women's issues" but issues of the church. One result of the segregation of these important issues is that they remain outside regular activities of the church, such as theological education, scriptural reflection, liturgical practice, and even worship. Another result is that leaders of the church can more easily avoid addressing these issues "seriously and responsibly."[3]

Ministers can also create awareness in Bible classes, premarital counseling sessions, marriage classes, marriage counseling sessions, youth programs, dating classes, children's classes, small-group meetings, and retreats. Domestic violence can be addressed in these informal or intimate settings, which provide a nonthreatening environment for victims, children, and abusers. Members can also be empowered to help friends, family, and neighbors whom they suspect are in abuse. A church that integrates abuse prevention and addresses family-violence issues will be a church that is healthy, evangelistic, and a light to the community.

Seminaries can require ministers to attend one or two workshops in domestic violence. Graduate schools can require reading for their students, that exposes them to domestic violence. Accreditation committees can push for abuse prevention to be part of the curriculum of all seminary students. Sin breeds in secret, but the light that shines into the darkness exposes evil. Awareness is a chance to expose, shed light on, and inform a congregation about evil in the world. When evil is acknowledged, it can be confronted. When we expose it, we can confront it and become the servants of King Jesus.

Confrontation

Once we have become aware of the problem and are creating awareness, then we go to the next step. That is, the church must confront the power structures of society. First, abuse must cease to exist in our families, culture, and communities. This is a big goal, but transforming cultures has always been the goal of Jesus. *Second,* after we have become aware of the problem, *we must be willing to confront abusers face to face.* Confronting abusers is risky, but it is the right thing to do. Abusers are manipulative, aggressive, and confusing, but the church must be confident.

---

3. Ibid., 11.

> When those of us in the church deny and ignore the potential for evil that resides in every person, we contribute to the church's failure to address evil in its most basic form and to provide leadership in confronting evil. When those of us in the church ignore evil in the world, we contribute to the church's failure to look at all of life, as well as to the church's collusion in propagating the delusion that the world is a safe and benevolent place. When the church fails to confront evil at any level, it ultimately robs those touched by evil of the faith resources for which they so desperately long.[4]

We in the church should protect victims and provide them with resources, rather than confronting them. They are not the ones who have been practicing sin. They have been surviving. Abusers are the ones who need to be confronted and challenged to stop their behavior.

Third, we must be willing to confront *the government and its leaders*. Ministers can take the lead by speaking out in their communities about abuse and domestic violence. They can also take the lead by providing a voice to the overworked, underpaid, and emotionally burdened victims' advocates. Law enforcement, government programs, and school systems all have decisions to make concerning their budgets and fiscal responsibility. Too often abuse-prevention programs are cut, because these organizations feel the need to conserve and work in a *crisis mode*. It is unfortunate that they do not devote ten years to prevention, with the realization that a generation could be changed as a result. Yet the reality is that our government agencies are financially stretched.

Fourth, the church must be willing to confront *shame by providing resources and hope for victims*. Domestic-violence victims and their children suffer tremendous scars and shame from their trauma and experiences. The church has the opportunity to enter their lives and aggressively love them and remind them that they have hope in God. We can empower them to become independent and to know that Jesus loves them. This can only happen when ministers take the first step. When preachers acknowledge that there is a problem, they begin the journey of reform in a world where abuse and domestic violence are epidemic. For far too long faith-community leaders have ignored the problem and hoped it would go away. It has not. It has continued to grow.

Why have ministers not addressed these issues? According to Al Miles, ministers do not get involved with addressing domestic violence because of 1) denial, 2) fear and helplessness, 3) lack of involvement in the issue, 4) misconceptions about abuse, 5) sexism in male ministers, and 6) lack of appropriate

---

4. Ibid., 10.

training.[5] Carol Goodman Kaufman also provides similar evidence in the Jewish community by suggesting that some rabbis: 1) feel that it is permissible to punish a woman, 2) deny that the problem exists in their synagogue, 3) try to defend the Jewish community as not having as big a problem as the rest of the world, or 4) feel helpless with the problem.[6] While both Miles and Kaufman indicate that there are clergy who confront abuse, the majority has fallen silent on the issue. "The magnitude of pastoral neglect . . . jolted me out of my own state of denial into reality. No longer could I think that pastors weren't coming to seminars on violence against women and children because they had scheduling conflicts or emergencies to tend to, the two most common excuses clergy had been giving me. I was forced to face the fact that many clergy people were willfully choosing to avoid these issues."[7]

This cannot be the case any longer. God has called faith communities to respond to the cries of the church. God has called faith community leaders to be God's voice and to move the community forward. The community must have leadership that is not afraid and that understands the heart of God. If the faith community will not do the work of God, then the government is left to do the divine task (Romans 13).

The Prophetic Church and Abuse

The prophetic church is one that calls the members and community to an awareness concerning the damage and dysfunction of domestic violence. The church, by creating awareness, can empower a community to take a stand against violence and help others to heal, forgive, and spiritually grow and develop. The prophetic church forms a community within its doors and outside in the local community. A community of peace and safety becomes a community that can seek God.

Second, the prophetic church, through awareness, becomes evangelistic. Too often churches try to avoid outside communities and see government workers as the enemy. The same can be true in how our communities view the church. Yet the prophetic church embraces the community and works together with the government to help eradicate violence and abuse. The prophetic church does not attempt to build its own shelters or raise its own money to help victims and abusers. The prophetic church does not create its own way of counseling batterers or victims. The prophetic church understands that God is active in our government, and that the service providers to victims

5. Miles, *Domestic Violence*, 153–55, 166–72.

6. Kaufman, *Sins of Omission*, 64–71.

7. Miles, *Domestic Violence*, 17–18.

and abusers are doing what we should have been doing for centuries. We in the churches should work together with advocates and counselors to provide families with the best resources possible. We should work with providers to offer spiritual counseling to families and should support the professionals who have devoted their lives to helping men and women caught in violence. Our outreach should be to all people, and we should let our communities know that God works through humans to advance the kingdom and bring peace to all families.

The church has a great opportunity to paint a picture for all victims, abusers, and children that provides them with hope and peace. Hope that they can be compassionate like God. Hope that we as a community are going to replace violence and control over others with empowerment and encouragement. Hope that people can change, and that love involves shared power and mutual respect and submission. Peace that comes when we live in hope and see our hope becoming reality. In the past, the church has not painted this vision for God's people. Jesus provided this vision and called the world to respond, but he depended on his disciples to carry this hope and vision to all people. Jesus's vision was for the world.

The movie *Kingdom Come* is an interesting portrayal of an African American family that has been affected by dysfunction and an abusive father. The father has passed away, and the children come home for the funeral. Conversations among the sons, daughters, mother, and other family members reflect the struggle they had experienced due to their father's behavior. The movie is a comedy, but it provides some valuable insights from a family scarred by abuse and dysfunction. One scene that I remember was a conversation between the widow, played by Whoopi Goldberg, and the minister, played by Cedric the Entertainer. The minister visits the widow and is concerned that she is angry with her husband. She tells him what she wants said at the funeral.

Goldberg's character wants "He was as mean as a snake" on her late husband's tombstone. While the minister encourages her to look at the positives in her husband's character, the widow feels that happier times were "few and far between." She continues to insist that the minister had not known her husband's true character and needs to be more honest. In the minister's attempt to be nice and to encourage forgiveness, the widow is not allowed to be angry and to see her husband for who he was. The minister, like many ministers, feels that forgiveness without repentance is important. Yet he does not understand that he is portraying a vision that is false and deceptive.

Kingdom Come tells a story about a family trying to heal from the affects of an abusive male. However, many of the characters outside the family try to prevent the children and spouse from accepting that they have been victims of an abuser and need to acknowledge their own pain, suffering, and humiliation in order to heal.

The church must portray a vision of hope, but we must also accept the truth and must teach others that God is a God of justice. We cannot give hope to victims by painting over the abuse and sin that they have suffered. We cannot help abusers heal if we do not address the problem and call them to change. Children will resent us if we redefine, deny, or minimize what they have seen. The vision must be one that deals with reality. We are providing a vision of hope to all people, not an illusion.

Our vision is that God calls all people into a relationship. Our vision is that God calls all people to repent. Our vision is that God wants all to be saved, safe, and at peace. Our vision is that God can transform anyone to be a man or woman of peace, mercy, and love. Our vision is that God is a God of justice and will protect the innocent and hold the oppressor accountable. Our vision is that we practice God's will on earth. Sometimes the vision brings fear; other times it brings joy. But always the *vision brings hope*!

Domestic violence is an epidemic in the United States as well as in the rest of the world. The statistics tell us that 25 percent of women have experienced physical or sexual abuse by an intimate partner.[8] The statistics for dating violence among teenage females are almost the same. One in six men has been sexually abused as children. Yet these statistics are only reported statistics and only involve physical abuse. It is possible that the numbers are higher when it comes to emotional and verbal abuse. We have a problem in our society with power and control issues, and it needs to stop.

If we take a theological view, God has addressed the problem. God is against oppression and stands for the rights of victims. God is a God of passion and mercy and has called the faith community to reflect this passion and mercy for victims. God has also called men to be like Jesus and to display the mercy, compassion, and courage that have been displayed in the ministry of Christ. God has called husbands and wives to live together in a covenant relationship that is healthy and supportive and that practices shared power. This relationship is shown by God's covenant with Israel and by Christ's relationship with the church.

This book has suggested that families caught in abuse develop a system of survival that is unhealthy for victims, children, and abusers. In the past,

---

8. Stark and Flitcraft, "Spouse Abuse."

churches and service providers have found it difficult to help the members of these families. Today providers are intervening, and empowering families to become healthy and to live with respect and love for one another. Unfortunately, many times the church's attempt to intervene has contributed to the problem. We have compounded the problems that victims face with our teachings concerning marriage, parenting, and victimization. We have missed the opportunity to empower victims to be free and to confront abusers and call them to repentance. We have failed to represent Christ in a world that seeks God. Our government has reflected the heart of God more than we have.

We now have two problems. One problem is the alarming presence of abuse, humiliation, and power and control in human relationships in our world and our churches. The other problem is the apathetic stance of the church in addressing abuse. God is addressing the first problem through the government agencies (Romans 13). God is addressing the second problem through other writers, ministers, theologians, and service providers whom I would call the modern prophets. Our legal system has responded to the first problem by providing aid, legal and emotional protection, and accountability to families in abuse. Has the church properly responded to the second problem? According to the modern prophets, the answer is NO!

> Many voices declare that the church has either caused men to be violent toward their wives or at least provided fertile soil for men's mistreatment of power within their families. They argue that since the church is part of the problem, it cannot be part of the solution. Thus when violence against women is being discussed, God's people are seldom consulted. Since we speak out so infrequently about violence, our collective voice is never heard on this issue. Generally speaking leaders in religious organizations and those involved in community pastoral care are never even invited to participate at the secular consultation table. The silence of our churches and our leaders is often interpreted in the public square as complicity with violent acts.[9]

> As long as Christian theology and pastoral practice do not publicly repent their collusion in sexual, domestic, and political violence against women and children, the victims of such violence are forced to choose between remaining a victim or remaining a Christian.[10]

> It is men's work to unlearn violence as a response to need, to learn to acknowledge and express needs in healthy, nonviolent ways, and to

9. Kroeger and Nason-Clark, *No Place for Abuse*, 16.
10. Fiorenza, "Introduction," xviii.

form relationships of intimacy and interdependence rather than dominance and control.[11]

The modern prophets have confronted the church for years, and we have slowly begun to respond. Will we continue to move forward, or will we fall behind? Will we respond, or will we continue to be silent?

The solution to this problem is to return to our Bibles, seek God in prayer and repentance, and be prophetic. The faith community must respond to the plight of victims by responding to the call of God. God has called the church to be prophetic, because God is a God of justice. The church must represent the heart of God and stand for the victims, the oppressed, and the afflicted. The church must also confront those who oppress, abuse, and humiliate others. God has not called us to have power over others; God has called us to empower and to practice shared power in our relationships. We have been called into covenant not only with God but also with each other. Our brothers and sisters should be living together in peace, compassion, and justice.

The church is to be prophetic by first creating awareness in our communities. We must acknowledge that abuse is a sin and that God wants it to stop. We must learn about the issue, and our preachers and teachers must address this in sermons, classes, and other venues. The church is then to confront evil, abusers, and our government and leadership structures that ignore the victims. The church must also confront shame by empowering victims to know they are loved and by calling abusers into a community of justice and love.

Finally, the church is to create a vision of hope for families in domestic violence. Preachers, like the prophets of old, have the power to paint pictures of hope with their words. Ministers should lead the way in proclaiming peace, hope, love, compassion, and above all, justice. With these messages, the church can be a light to the community. The church can call government workers to endure, persevere, and practice justice. The church can call government leaders to make their budgets with hope and faith that prevention is the best medicine. The church can provide victims with hope that God and the disciples of Jesus do hear their cries. The church can remind abusers that God is not blind, and that the risen Lord is a God of justice and power. The church can provide families with a healthy model of covenant and parental support. The church can remind the world once again that God is with us.

This begins with you. Hopefully you have learned something in reading this book that will provoke a response. This book is not intended to be a complete guide to working with abuse, but it is intended to start the conversation.

11. Cooper-White, *The Cry of Tamar*, 218.

It is intended to move the minister to decide to investigate. I challenge and encourage you, one prophet to another, to do the following:

1. Read some of the books listed below and others listed in the bibliography:

   » Bancroft, Lundy. *Why Does He Do That? Inside the Minds of Angry and Controlling Men*. New York: Berkley, 2003.

   » Clark, Ron. *Setting the Captives Free: A Christian Theology of Domestic Abuse*. Eugene, OR: Cascade Books, 2005.

   » Engel, Beverly. *The Emotionally Abused Woman: Overcoming Destructive Patterns and Reclaiming Yourself*. New York: Fawcett Columbine, 1990.

   » Kroeger, Catherine Clark, and Nancy Nason-Clark. *No Place for Abuse: Biblical and Practical Resources to Counteract Domestic Violence*. Downer's Grove, IL: InterVarsity, 2001.

   » Livingston, David J. *Healing Violent Men: A Model for Christian Communities*. Minneapolis: Fortress, 2002.

   » Miles, Al. *Domestic Violence: What Every Pastor Needs to Know*. Minneapolis: Fortress, 2000.

   » Nason-Clark, Nancy. *The Battered Wife: How Christians Confront Family Violence*. Louisville: Westminster John Knox, 1997.

2. Attend a domestic-violence intervention training, and view one video or movie concerning abuse.

3. If you are a minister, commit to preaching one sermon in the next three months devoted to addressing domestic violence. If you are not a minister, encourage your minister to address the issue. Pray with and for your ministers, and urge them to become aware of the problem.

4. Offer to start a reading group in your congregation that reads books written by survivors and that discuss the issues of power and control. A reading list for such a group might include the following:

   » Evans, Patricia. *The Verbally Abusive Relationship: How to Recognize it and How to Respond*. Expanded 2nd ed. Holbrook, MA: Adams Media Corporation, 1996.

   » Weldon, Michelle. *I Closed My Eyes: Revelations of a Battered Woman*. Center City, MN: Hazelden, 1999.

5. Invite a domestic-violence intervention advocate to speak to your group about intimate-partner violence.

6. Never get in over your head! Always refer victims and abusers to professional counselors or advocates. For the victim's safety, as well as your own, make sure she is getting the best help possible. Working with advocates can build a strong support bridge for the victim to cross in her journey to peace, safety, and healing.

If you are a minister, preaching on this subject will be a great experience for you. The first sermon I gave on abuse was well supported by the congregation. One young couple was visiting that morning. Three months later, I baptized the young woman, and she told me she had left her husband because he was abusive. After my earlier sermon, the woman told me, her husband had accused her of telling me about their problem and had beat her that afternoon. I was crushed. I said, "I am so sorry. If I would have known—" She interrupted, "No, I am glad you did it. I never knew how God felt till then. You keep preaching about it." Since then, many women who sit by their abusive husbands in church have told me the same thing: "My husband doesn't like this . . ." Or, "My husband thinks you talk too much about social justice and abuse . . ." They all end with the same statement, however: "Keep preaching about it." Who would have thought that those who are oppressed and afflicted would be the ones to encourage the preacher!

This is my advice to you. When you come to understand how God feels about domestic violence, keep preaching, teaching, and telling others about it. You will see a great blessing in your ministries, not because of you, but because those who seek God will be given what they need. God will lead victims, abusers, children, and domestic-violence workers into the congregation. Those affected by domestic violence need support, hope, and justice. To whom will God send them?

How beautiful are the feet of those who preach good news! (Rom 10:15; cf. Isa 52:7)

Bibliography

Adams, Carol J. *Woman-Battering*. Creative Pastoral Care and Counseling Series. Minneapolis: Fortress, 1994.

Amato, Paul R., and Alan Booth. "Consequences of Parental Divorce and Marital Unhappiness for Adult Well-Being." *Social Forces* 69 (1991) 895–914.

Anderson, Ray S. *The Shape of Practical Theology: Empowering Ministry with Theological Praxis*. Downers Grove, IL: InterVarsity, 2001.

Bancroft, Lundy, and Jay G. Silverman. *The Batterer as Parent: Addressing the Impact of Domestic Violence on Family Dynamics*. Sage Series on Violence against Women. Thousand Oaks: Sage, 2002.

Bancroft. *When Dad Hurts Mom: Helping Your Children Heal the Wounds of Witnessing Abuse*. New York: Putnam, 2004.

———. *Why Does He Do That? Inside the Minds of Angry and Controlling Men*. New York: Berkley, 2003.

Becvar, Dorothy Stroh, and Raphael J. Becvar. *Family Therapy: A Systemic Integration*. 2nd ed. Boston: Allyn & Bacon, 1993.

Berlin, Adele, et al., editors. *The Jewish Study Bible: Tanakh Translation*. New York: Oxford University Press, 2004.

Bevan, Emma, and Daryl J. Higgins. "Is Domestic Violence Learned? The Contribution of Five Forms of Child Maltreatment to Men's Violence and Adjustment." *Journal of Family Violence* 17 (2002) 223–45.

Boston Medical Center Pediatrics. "Child Witness to Violence Project." Online: www .childwitnesstoviolence.org/care_givers/for_aregivers_facts.html.

Boyd, Gregory A. *Is God to Blame? Beyond Pat Answers to the Problem of Suffering*. Downers Grove, IL: InterVarsity, 2003.

Burch, Rebecca L., and Gordon G. Gallup Jr. "Pregnancy as a Stimulus for Domestic Violence." *Journal of Family Violence* 19 (2004) 243–47.

Campbell, Jacquelyn. "Correlates of Battering during Pregnancy." *Research Nursing Health* 15 (1992) 219–26.

———. "Why Battering during Pregnancy?" *Clinical Issues in Perinatal and Health Nursing* 4 (1993) 343–49.

Clark, Ron. "Kingdoms, Kids, and Kindness: A New Look at Luke 18:15–17." *Stone Campbell Journal* 2 (2002) 81–98.

———. "Open Your Eyes." *Journal of Religion and Abuse* 4:1 (2002) 27–36.

———. *Setting the Captives Free: A Christian Theology for Domestic Abuse*. Eugene, OR: Cascade Books, 2005.

———. "The Silence in Dinah's Cry: Narrative in Genesis 34 in a Context of Sexual Violence." *Journal of Religion and Abuse* 2 (2001) 81–98.

Clements, Caroline M., et al. "Dysphoria and Hopelessness Following Battering: The Role of Perceived Control, Coping, and Self-Esteem." *Journal of Family Violence* 19 (2004) 25–36.

Dahlberg, Gunilla. "The Parent-Child Relationship and Socialization in the Context of Modern Childhood: The Case of Sweden." In *Parent-Child Socialization in Diverse Cultures*, edited by Jaipaul L. Roopnarine and D. Bruce Carter, 121–37. Annual Advances in Applied Developmental Psychology 5. Norwood, NJ: Ablex, 1992.

Dixon, Cynthia. "Clergy as Carers: A Response to the Pastoral Concern of Violence in the Family." *Journal of Psychology and Christianity* 16 (1997) 126–31.

Dugan, Meg Kennedy, and Roger R. Hock. *It's My Life Now: Starting Over after an Abusive Relationship of Domestic Violence*. New York: Routledge, 2000.

Eldredge, John. *Wild at Heart: Discovering the Passionate Soul of a Man*. Nashville: Thomas Nelson, 2001.

Elliger, Karl, et al., editors. *Biblia Hebraica Stuttgartensia*. Stuttgart: Deutsche Biblestiftung, 1977.

Engel, Beverly. *The Emotionally Abused Woman: Overcoming Destructive Patterns and Reclaiming Yourself*. New York: Fawcett Columbine, 1990.

Engel, Mary Patten. "Historical Theology and Violence against Women: Unearthing a Popular Tradition of Just Battery." In *Violence against Women and Children: A Christian Theological Sourcebook*, edited by Carol J. Adams and Marie M. Fortune, 242–61. New York: Continuum, 1998.

Erickson, Millard J. *Christian Theology*. 2nd ed. Grand Rapids: Baker, 1999.

Estrella, Rosa Emily Nina. "Effects of Violence on Interpersonal Relations and Strategies That Promote Family Unity." Paper presented at La Familia Unida: La Fuerza del Futuro. Fourth annual Power in Partnership Bilingual Conference. Portland, OR, June 20, 2003.

Evans, Patricia. *The Verbally Abusive Relationship: How to Recognize It and How to Respond*. 2nd ed. Holbrook, MA: Adams Media Corporation, 1996.

Fiorenza, Elisabeth Schüssler. "Introduction." In *Violence against Women*, edited by Elizabeth Schüssler Fiorenza and M. Shawn Copeland, vii–xxiv. Concilium 1994/1. Maryknoll: Orbis, 1994.

Fortune, Marie M. "The Transformation of Suffering: A Biblical and Theological Perspective." In *Christianity, Patriarchy, and Abuse: A Feminist Critique*, edited by Joanne Carlson Brown and Carole R. Bon, 139–47. New York: Pilgrim, 1989.

Garbardi, Lisa, and Lee. A. Rosen. "Intimate Relationships: College Students from Divorced and Intact Families." *Journal of Divorce and Remarriage* 18 (1993) 25–56.

Gill-Austern, Brita L. "Love Understood as Self-Sacrifice and Self-Denial: What Does It Do to Women?" In *Through the Eyes of Women: Insights for Pastoral Care*, edited by Jeanne Stevenson Moessner, 304–21. Minneapolis: Fortress, 1996.

Gray, John. *Men Are from Mars, Women Are from Venus: A Practical Guide for Improving Communication and Getting What You Want in Your Relationship*. New York: HarperCollins, 1992.

Grenz, Stanley J. *Theology for the Community of God*. Grand Rapids: Eerdmans, 2000.

Hamby, Sherry L. "Acts of Psychological Aggression against a Partner and Their Relation to Physical Assault and Gender." *Journal of Marriage and the Family* 61 (1999) 959–70.

Hansen, Christine. "A Considerate Service: An Advocate's Introduction to Domestic Violence and the Military." *Domestic Violence Report* 6 (2001) 1–6.

Harland, Philip A. *Associations, Synagogues, and Congregations: Claiming a Place in Ancient Mediterranean Society.* Minneapolis: Fortress, 2003.

Heise, Lori, et al. "Ending Violence against Women." Population Reports, Series L, No. 11. Baltimore: Johns Hopkins University School of Public Health, Population Information Program, December 1999. Online: http://www.infoforhealth.org/pr/l11/l11creds.shtml#top/

Hellerman, Joseph H. *The Ancient Church as Family.* Minneapolis: Fortress, 2001.

Instone-Brewer, David. *Divorce and Remarriage in the Bible: The Social and Literary Context.* Grand Rapids: Eerdmans, 2002.

Jhally, Sut, director. *Tough Guise: Violence, Media, and the Crisis in Masculinity.* VHS Videocassette. Northampton, MA: Media Education Foundation, 1999.

Johnson, John M., and Denise M. Bondurant. "Revisiting the 1982 Church Response Survey. In *Violence against Women and Children: A Christian Theological Sourcebook*, edited by Carol J. Adams and Marie M. Fortune, 422–27. New York: Continuum, 1998.

Jouriles, Ernest N., et al. "Knives, Guns, and Interparent Violence: Relations with Child Behavior Problems." *Journal of Family Psychology* 12 (1998) 178–94.

Kaufman, Carol Goodman. *Sins of Omission: The Jewish Commuinity's Reaction to Domestic Violence.* Boulder, CO: Westview, 2003.

Kelman, Herbert C. "Reconiciliation as Identity Change: A Social-Psychological Perspective." In *From Conflict Resolution to Reconciliation*, edited by Yocaav Bar-Siman-Tov, 111–24. New York: Oxford University Press, 2004.

Kerr, Michael E., and Murray Bowen. *Family Evaluation: An Approach Based on Bowden Theory.* New York: Norton, 1988.

Ketterman, Grace. *Verbal Abuse: Healing the Hidden Wound.* Ann Arbor: Servant, 1992.

Kivel, Paul. *Men's Work: How to Stop the Violence That Tears Our Lives Apart.* Center City, MN: Hazeldon, 1992.

———. "Paul Kivel: Violence Prevention Educator." Web site. Online: http://www.paulkivel.com/

Kroeger, Catherine Clark, and Nancy Nason-Clark. *No Place for Abuse: Biblical and Practical Resources to Counteract Domestic Violence.* Downers Grove, IL: InterVarsity, 2001.

Livingston, David J. *Healing Violent Men: A Model for Christian Communities.* Minneapolis: Fortress, 2002.

Mananzan, Mary John. "Feminine Socialization: Women as Victims and Collaborators." In *Violence against Women*, edited by Elisabeth Schüssler Fiorenza and M. Shawn Copeland, 44–52. Maryknoll: Orbis, 1994.

Martin, Grant L. *Critical Problems in Children and Youth: Counseling Techniques for Problems Resulting from Attention Deficit Disorder, Sexual Abuse, Custody Battles, and Related Issues.* Contemporary Christian Counseling 5. Waco, TX: Word, 1992.

Martin, Sandra L., et al. "Changes in Intimate Partner Violence during Pregnancy." *Journal of Family Violence* 19 (2004) 201–10.

Mathews, Alice P. *Preaching that Speaks to Women.* Grand Rapids: Baker, 2003.

McClintock, Karen A. *Sexual Shame: An Urgent Call to Healing.* Minneapolis: Fortress, 2001.

Means, J. Jeffrey., with contributions from Mary Ann Nelson. *Trauma & Evil: Healing the Wounded Soul*. Minneapolis: Fortress, 2000.

Miles, Al. *Domestic Violence: What Every Pastor Needs to Know*. Minneapolis: Fortress, 2000.

Miller, Mary Susan. *No Visible Wounds: Identifying Nonphysical Abuse of Women by Their Men*. New York: Random House, 1995.

Multnomah County Health Department, et al. *Domestic Violence in Multnomah County*. February 2000. Online: http://www.co.multnomah.or.us/dchs/dv/report .shtml/.

Murphy, Jeffrie G. *Getting Even: Forgiveness and Its Limits*. New York: Oxford University Press, 2003.

Nason-Clark, Nancy. *The Battered Wife: How Christians Confront Family Violence*. Louisville: Westminster John Knox, 1997.

Nestle, Eberhard et al, editors. *Novum Testamentum Graeca*. 27th ed. Stuttgart: Deutsche Bibelgesellschaft, 1993.

Poling, James Newton. *The Abuse of Power: A Theological Problem*. Nashville: Abingdon, 1991.

Porter, Stanley F. *"Katallasso" in Ancient Greek Literature, with Reference to the Pauline Writings*. Estudios de Filología Neotestamentaria 5. Cordoba, Spain: Ediciones El Almendro, 1994.

Rennison, Callie Marie. *Intimate Partner Violence from 1993 to 2001*. Bureau of Justice Statistics Crime Data Brief. Online: http://www.ojp.usdoj.gov/bjs/pub/pdf/ipv01 .pdf/.

Rennison, Callie Marie, and Sarah Welchans. *Intimate Partner Violence*. Bureau of Justice Statistics Special Report (May 2000). Online: http://www.ojp.usdoj.gov/ bjs/pub/pdf/ipv.pdf/.

Richardson, Ron. *Creating a Healthier Church: Family Systems Theory, Leadership, and Congregational Life*. Creative Pastoral Care and Counseling Series. Minneapolis: Fortress, 1996.

Schimmel, Solomon. *Wounds Not Healed by Time: The Power of Repentance and Forgiveness*. New York: Oxford University Press, 2002.

Simons, Ronald L., et al. "Socialization in the Family of Origin and Male Dating Violence: A Prospective Study." *Journal of Marriage and the Family* 60 (1998) 467–78.

Smith, Mark. *The Origins of Biblical Monotheism: Israel's Polytheistic Background and the Ugaritic Texts*. New York: Oxford University Press, 2001.

Stark, Evan, and Anne H. Flitcraft. "Spouse Abuse." In *Violence in America: A Public Health Approach*, edited by Mark L. Rosenberg and Mary Ann Fenley, 123–57. Surgeon General's Workshop on Violence and Public Health (1985: Leesburg, Virginia). New York: Oxford University Press, 1991.

Straton, Jack C. "What Is Fair for Children of Abusive Men?" *Journal of the Task Group on Child Custody Issues of the National Organization for Men against Sexism* 5 (2001) 1–10.

Szegedy-Maszak, Marianne. "Death at Fort Bragg." *U.S. News and World Report*, August 12, 2002, 44.

———. "Physical Assault on Women by an Intimate Male Partner, Selected Population-Based Studies, 1982–99, Table 1." *Population Report Series L: Number* 11. Online: www.infoforhealth.org/pr/L11/L11tables.shtml.

Talbot, Jennifer. "Children Witnessing Domestic Violence." Paper presented at the "Working with Abusive Men" workshop. Portland State University, Portland, OR, May 2002.

Tavris, Carol. *Anger: The Misunderstood Emotion* Rev. ed. New York: Simon & Schuster, 1989.

Thompson, Barbara. "An Interview with James Garbarino on the Impact of Violence on Children." *World Vision* (April–May 1995) 8–9.

Tjaden, Patricia, and Nancy Thoennes. *Full Report of the Prevalence, Incidence, and Consequences of Intimate Partner Violence against Women: Findings from the National Violence against Women Survey.* Washington DC: U.S. Department of Justice, Office of Justice Programs, National Institute of Justice, 2000.

Tripolitis, Antonia. *Religions of the Hellenistic Roman Age.* Grand Rapids: Eerdmans, 2002.

Weitzman, Susan. *"Not to People Like Us": Hidden Abuse in Upscale Marriages.* New York: Basic Books, 2000.

Weldon, Michelle. *I Closed My Eyes: Revelations of a Battered Woman.* Center City, MN: Hazelden, 1999.

White, Pamela Cooper. *The Cry of Tamar: Violence against Women and the Church's Response.* Minneapolis: Fortress, 1995.

Winter, Bruce W. *Roman Wives, Roman Widows: The Appearance of New Women and the Pauline Community.* Grand Rapids: Eerdmans, 2003.

Scripture Index

Old Testament

Genesis

1:26	58
1:27–28	69
2	90
2:18	58
2:20b–25	90
2:24	74
6:6	32
8:21	57
34	37, 135

Exodus

4:16	51
4:31	21
15:3	29
22:21	61
22:22–24	60
32:11	32
32:14	32
34:6–7	32, 56

Leviticus

20	135

Numbers

11:1	32

Deuteronomy

7:7–9	58
7:9–11	82
7:9	56–57
27	135

Judges

19	135

2 Samuel

13	135

1 Kings

21:28–29	58

2 Kings

23:13	69

Job

1–2	59
1:21b	123

Psalms

9:9	60
95:1–9	24

Proverbs

11:14	55
12:15	55, 108
14:31	61
15:22	55, 108
17:5	60
21:13	75, 110
23:10–11	61
30:18–19	16

Isaiah

1:21–23	87
50:1	83, 86
52:5	83
54:6–7	82–83, 86
54:6	58
63:10	124
66:9	69
66:13	69